RELATIONAL DATABASE SYSTEMS

A Pragmatic Approach

GW00372647

INFORMATION SYSTEMS SERIES

Consulting Editors

D. E. AVISON
BA, MSc, PHD, FBCS
*Department of Computer Science and
Applied Mathematics, Aston University,
Birmingham, UK*

G. FITZGERALD
BA, MSc, MBCS
*Oxford Institute of Information Management
Templeton College, Oxford, UK*

This series of student texts covers a wide variety of topics relating to information systems. It is designed to fulfil the needs of the growing number of courses on, and interest in, computing and information systems which do not focus on the purely technological aspects, but seek to relate these to business or organisational context.

Relational Database Systems: A Pragmatic Approach

PAUL BEYNON-DAVIES BSc (Econ.), PHD, MBCS
The Polytechnic of Wales

OXFORD
BSP PROFESSIONAL BOOKS
LONDON EDINBURGH BOSTON
MELBOURNE PARIS BERLIN VIENNA

© Paul Beynon-Davies 1991

Blackwell Scientific Publications
Editorial offices:
Osney Mead, Oxford OX2 0EL
25 John Street, London WC1N 2BL
23 Ainslie Place, Edinburgh EH3 6AJ
3 Cambridge Center, Cambridge,
    Massachusetts 02142, USA
54 University Street, Carlton
    Victoria 3053, Australia

Other Editorial Offices:
Arnette SA
2, rue Casimir-Delavigne
75006 Paris
France

Blackwell Wissenschaft
Meinekestrasse 4
D-1000 Berlin 15
Germany

Blackwell MZV
Feldgasse 13
A-1238 Wien
Austria

First published 1991

Printed and bound in Great Britain by
Hartnolls Ltd, Bodmin, Cornwall

DISTRIBUTORS

Marston Book Services Ltd
PO Box 87
Oxford OX2 0DT
(*Orders*: Tel: 0865 791155
        Fax: 0865 791927
        Telex: 837515)

USA
Blackwell Scientific Publications, Inc.
3 Cambridge Center
Cambridge, MA 02142
(*Orders*: Tel: 800 759-6102)

Canada
Oxford University Press
70 Wynford Drive
Don Mills
Ontario M3C 1J9
(*Orders*: Tel: 416 441-2941)

Australia
Blackwell Scientific Publications
(Australia) Pty Ltd
54 University Street
Carlton, Victoria 3053
(*Orders*: Tel: 03 347-0300)

British Library
Cataloguing in Publication Data

Beynon-Davies, Paul
    Relational database systems: a pragmatic approach.—
    (Information systems series)
    1. Relational databases
    I. Title.   II. Series
    005.756

ISBN 0-632-03116-6

Library of Congress
Cataloging in Publications Data

Beynon-Davies, Paul
    Relational database systems: a pragmatic approach/
    Paul Beynon-Davies
        p.   cm.—(Information systems series)
    Includes bibliographical references and index.
    ISBN 0-632-03116-6
    1. Relational data bases.
    I. Title.   II. Series: Information systems series (Oxford, England)
    QA76.9.D3B49   1991
    005.75'6—dc20

For my Mother and Father,
David Beynon Davies and Enid Yvonne Thomas

Contents

6   Data Analysis   94

7   Application Development   107

Foreword

The Blackwell Scientific Publications Series on Information Systems is a series of student texts covering a wide variety of topics relating to information systems. It is designed to fulfil the needs of the growing number of courses on, and interest in, computing and information systems which do not focus on the purely technological aspects, but seek to relate these to the business and organisational context.

The information systems area has been defined as the effective design, delivery, use and impact of information technology in organisations and society. Utilising this fairly wide definition, it is clear that the subject area is somewhat interdisciplinary. Thus the series seeks to integrate technological disciplines with management and other disciplines, for example, psychology and philosophy. It is felt that these areas do not have a natural home, they are rarely represented by single departments in polytechnics and universities, and to put such books into a purely computer science or management series restricts potential readership and the benefits that such texts can provide. This series on information systems now provides such a home.

The books will be mainly student texts, although certain topics may be dealt with at a deeper, more research-oriented level.

The series is expected to include the following areas, although this is not an exhaustive list: information systems development methodologies, office information systems, management information systems, decision support systems, information modelling and databases, systems theory, human aspects and the human-computer interface, application systems, technology strategy, planning and control, and expert systems, knowledge acquisition and representation.

A mention of the books so far published in the series gives a 'flavour' of the richness of the information systems world. *Information Systems Development: Methodologies, Techniques and Tools* (D.E. Avison and G. Fitzgerald), looks at many of the areas discussed above in overview form; *Information and Data Modelling* (D. Benyon), concerns itself with one very important aspect, the world of data, in some depth; *Structured Systems Analysis and Design Methods* (G. Cutts) looks at one particular information systems development methodology in detail; and *Multiview: An Exploration in Information Systems Development* (D.E. Avison and A.T. Wood-Harper) is a contingency approach to information systems development which incorporates, amongst other influences, soft systems and socio-technical views in its framework. *Information Systems Research: Issues, Techniques and Practical Guidelines* (R. Galliers (ed.)) provides a collection of papers on key information systems; *Organisations and Information Technology, Systems, Power and Job Design* (I. Winfield) critically examines the impact of information technology on organisations and reviews good and bad practice; and *Software Engineering for Information Systems* (D. McDermid) discusses software engineering in the context of information systems. There are a number of other titles in preparation.

This new book by Paul Beynon-Davies gives the reader a practical approach to databases and is a very useful companion to David Benyon's book in the series. Relational databases are the most widespread of database systems in use, and amongst these ORACLE is the most widely used product. Beynon-Davies sets the database scene by reviewing the theoretical ideas behind relational databases and then examines the practical consequences of these, using SQL (Structured Query Language) and ORACLE to highlight the strengths and weaknesses of the current facilities. The major components of data definition, data manipulation, integrity and control are examined in separate chapters, and there are two chapters looking at data analysis and application development so that the reader can see how a database application may develop. He also considers the future developments in this area. This text will be an excellent introductory course book into the exciting world of databases.

David Avison and Guy Fitzgerald
Joint Consulting Editors
Information Systems Series

Preface

Mission Statement

In recent years, databases, particularly relational databases, have ceased to be an advanced topic for Computer Studies students. Instead, the topic has become a standard one, typically offered in the first or second years of a degree and even on Higher National Diploma courses. The style of the current work is clearly directed at this change of emphasis. Rather than acting as a major work of reference running into encyclopaedic proportions it aims to offer a conceptually clear-cut, tutorial guide to the subject. This it does via some well-thought-out examples, an armoury of tried-and-tested illustrations, numerous problems with sample solutions, and a developed case study.

Most existing literature on Relational Databases is far more about the theory of the Relational Data Model than the practice of Relational Databases. The word *practice* is frequently interpreted in the sense in which books devote attention to the intricacies of database design via techniques such as Entity-Relationship Diagramming and Normalisation. This however is a rather narrow interpretation. These topics are very important, and warrant a complementary book to themselves, but at least as important is a discussion of at least one representative Relational Database Management System (RDBMS). The present work therefore uses ORACLE, probably the most widely used RDBMS in the commercial world, to illustrate the use of relational kernel/toolkit products for information systems development.

Recently E.F. Codd, the founder of the relational database movement, has described his work as an attempt to formulate a detailed description of an abstract machine for database work (Codd 1990). The main advantage of an abstraction is that by its very nature it is buffered from implementation detail. An abstract machine can be implemented in many different ways in hardware, software or both. Codd wishes his abstract machine description to be treated by all database vendors, standards committees and database users as an abstract machine standard.

Codd has continually been at odds however with database vendors, standards committees and indeed many database users. Although many see him as a gifted theoretician who continually lays the groundwork for the practical database work of the future, others see him as an ivory tower critic of successful contemporary database work. Whatever your opinion, E.F. Codd and a range of others have been successful at fostering a much-needed debate in the database world. This debate is dialectical in the sense that the conflict between theoretical formalism and actual database products fuses a continual synthesis in hopefully better and better tools for data management.

Pragmatism is frequently defined as being a philosophy or philosophical method that makes practical consequences the test of truth. At first glance, the title of the present work might seem to place the author in the camp of relational database vendors sneering at the disparaging criticisms of Messrs. Codd and Co. On the contrary, the author has aimed to provide a readable introduction to the Relational controversy. This is achieved primarily through a continual contrast between the theoretician's abstract machine or Data Model and the developing nature of relational database practice as embodied in a database sub-language known as SQL. The aim then is to examine the practical consequences of the theoretician's ideas, and highlight these against the contemporary facilities for relational database work.

This approach serves as a useful anchor for not only gaining a thorough understanding of the contemporary relational scene, but is also extremely useful for pinpointing some likely strands of future database development.

Overview of the Book

Chapter 1 is a definitional chapter. Here we examine the development of the database idea. We set some initial definitions for the terms Database, Data Model and Database Management System (DBMS) and briefly review the standard database sub-language SQL.

In the first chapter we also outline the characteristics of the abstract machine proposed by Codd. This machine, or Data Model, is generally held to have three parts: data definition, data manipulation and data integrity. To this we add a fourth part, data control, which through much emphasis in database products has now become established in the theoretical literature (Codd, 1990). This is just one example of the dialectical nature of the relational scene referred to above.

Chapters 2, 3, 4 and 5 discuss in some depth these four parts of the relational data model. Each chapter begins with an examination of a part of the abstract machine portrayed by Codd and others. This is then contrasted against the way in which data definition, data manipulation, data integrity and data control is handled in SQL. The SQL discussed is primarily taken from the ISO standards document (ISO, 1987). Where the discussion turns to the realm of the specifics of ORACLE's implementation of SQL or to enhancements to the 1987 standard this is indicated.

A great deal of literature on database design has grown up around the Relational Data Model. Chapter 6 acts in the capacity of an introduction to this material.

Chapter 7 moves from design to implementation. It reviews the way in which a database is now commonly the core around which a whole toolkit of information system building products have developed.

Chapter 8 concludes by summing up the relational controversy and looking at some contrasting and complementary approaches to database work which look like influencing development patterns in the short-term and long-term future.

The appendices are used to enhance the discussion of the main body of text. Appendix 1 discusses one of the big question marks that has been placed over the head of relational databases - the question of performance. Appendix 2 is designed as an informal source of reference for the main version of SQL discussed in the book. Appendix 3 represents an overview of a number of rules provided by E.F. Codd for assessing whether or not a given DBMS can be truly called relational. Finally, appendix 4 contains an extended case study which illustrates the development of a given application in a relational database.

Chapter 1
Databases, Data Models and Database Management Systems

1.1 The Data Problem

Most of the information systems developed on early business computers were developed in a piecemeal or ad-hoc manner. Manual systems were analysed, redesigned and transferred onto the computer with little thought to their position within the organisation as a whole.

This piecemeal approach by definition produces a number of separate information systems, each with its own program suite, its own files, and its own inputs and outputs. As a result, the systems by themselves

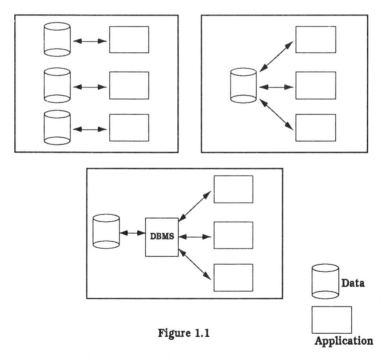

Figure 1.1

do not represent the way in which the organisation works, ie, as a complex set of interacting and interdependent systems.

Because of the many problems inherent in the piecemeal approach, it is nowadays considered desirable to maintain a single centralised pool of organisational data, rather than a series of separate files. Such a pool of data is known as a database.

It is also considered desirable to integrate the systems that use this data around a piece of software which manages all interactions with the database. Such a piece of software is known as a database management system or DBMS. Figure 1.1 illustrates these developments.

1.2 What is a Database?

A database in manual terms is analogous to a filing cabinet, or more accurately to a series of filing cabinets. A database is an organised repository for data. The overall purpose of such a system is to maintain data for some set of enterprise objectives. Normally, such objectives fall within the domain of business administration. Most database systems are built to retain the data required for the running of the

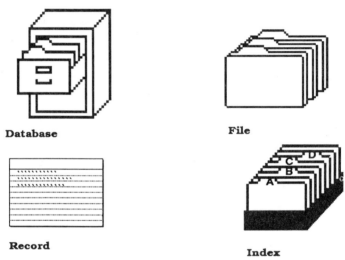

Database

File

Record

Index

Figure 1.2

day-to-day activities of a business.

Organisation usually implies some logical division, usually hierarchical. Hence we speak of a database as being a collection of files. A collection of files containing information on company employees, for instance, would normally constitute a database. Each file in a database is in turn also a structured collection of data. In manual terms, such files would be folders hung in a filing cabinet. Each file in the cabinet consists of a series of records. These might be cards of information, for example, on each employee in a company. Figure 1.2 illustrates the physical representation of the concepts of database, file, record and index.

Each employee record, like the one illustrated in figure 1.3, is divided up into a series of areas known as fields. Within each field a specific value is written. Occasionally we may wish to retrieve information about a given employee quickly. For this purpose we maintain a card index which might store, for instance, the names of employees arranged in alphabetical order together with a reference to the physical location of the record for a given employee.

We shall encounter these terms again and again throughout this work. One of the major advantages of the relational approach to data is that it closely emulates the traditional physical organisation of data described above.

But what organisational purpose does a database serve? A database can be viewed as a model of reality. The information stored in a database is usually an attempt to represent the properties of some objects in the real world. Hence, for instance, a personnel database is meant to record relevant details of people. We say relevant, because no database can store all the properties of real-world objects. A database is therefore an

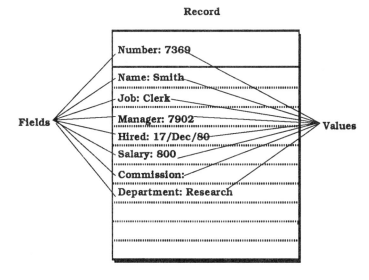

Figure 1.3

abstraction of the real world. We shall return to this important issue of abstraction in chapter 8.

1.3 Properties of a Database

The question of organisation is therefore of fundamental importance to a database system. In database terms organisation further implies a series of properties:

(1)   Data Sharing
(2)   Data Integration
(3)   Data Integrity
(4)   Data Security
(5)   Data Abstraction
(6)   Data Independence

1.3.1 Data Sharing

Database systems were originally developed for use within multi-user environments. In such environments, data held in a database is not usually there solely for the use of one person. A database is normally accessible by more than one person perhaps at the same time. Hence our personnel database might be accessible by members of not only the personnel department but also the payroll department.

1.3.2 Data Integration

Shared data brings numerous advantages to the organisation. Such advantages, however, only result if the database is treated responsibly. One major responsibility of database usage is to ensure that the data is integrated. This implies that a database should be a collection of data which has no unnecessarily duplicated or redundant data. In the past, separate personnel and payroll systems maintained similar data on company employees such as names, addresses, dates of birth etc. The aim of a database system is to store one logical item of data in one place only.

1.3.3 Data Integrity

Another responsibility arising as a consequence of shared data is that a database should display integrity. In other words, that the database accurately reflects the universe of discourse it is attempting to model. This means that if relationships exist in the real world between objects represented by data in our database then changes made to one partner in such a relationship should be accurately reflected in changes made to other partners in that relationship. Hence, if changes are made to the information stored on a particular company department, for instance, then relevant changes should be made to the information stored on employees of that department.

1.3.4 Data Security

One of the major ways of ensuring the integrity of a database is by restricting access. In other words, securing the database. The major way this is done in contemporary database systems is by defining in some detail a set of authorised users of the whole, or more usually parts of the database. A secure system would be one where the payroll department has access to information for the production of salaries but is prohibited from changing the pay points of company employees. This activity is the sole responsibility of the personnel department.

1.3.5 Data Abstraction

Database systems are high-level tools. They are abstraction tools. As we shall discuss in chapter 8, more and more emphasis has been placed on the database concept as a conceptual modelling tool. The major theme underlying database work is the attempt to model the logical structure of data and separate this from any physical implementation concerns.

1.3.6 Data Independence

One immediate consequence of abstraction is the idea of buffering data from the processes that use such data. The ideal is to achieve a situation where data organisation is transparent to the users or application programs which feed off data. If, for instance, a change is made to some part of the underlying database no application programs using affected data should need to be changed. Also, if a change is made to some part of an application system then this should not affect the structure of the underlying data used by the application.

1.4 What is a Database Management System?

To use our manual office analogy again, whereas a database may be conceived of as one or more filing cabinets, a Database Management System or DBMS is analogous to an established set of procedures and mechanisms for maintaining such filing cabinets. A DBMS constitutes knowledge about the underlying structure of stored data and established procedures for:

(1)   adding new files to the database
(2)   removing files from the database
(3)   restricting access to files in the database
(4)   inserting new data into existing files
(5)   updating data in existing files
(6)   deleting data from existing files

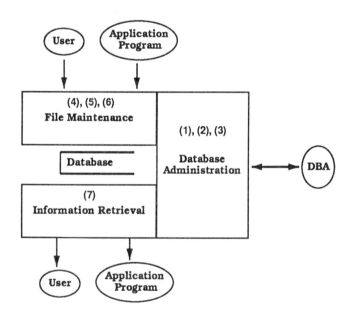

Figure 1.4

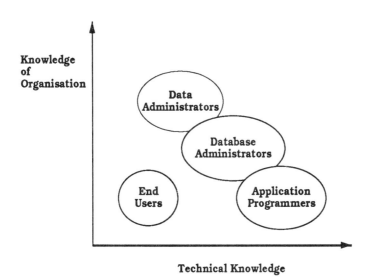

Figure 1.5

(7)   retrieving data from existing files.

Procedures 1 to 3 are normally encapsulated in the term database administration. Procedures 4 to 6 are normally referred to as file maintenance procedures. Procedure 7 is frequently classed as information retrieval. Figure 1.4 illustrates the interaction between these three major areas of database management.

1.5 Users of Database Systems

Since a database is designed to be a centralised store of organisational data, the users of such a system are likely to come from a diverse pool. Figure 1.5 identifies four key roles to be found interacting with most database systems. Each role is plotted against the two dimensions of knowledge of the organisation and technical knowledge.

The average end-user will have little technical knowledge of operating systems and DBMS, but he or she will have a large amount of knowledge about the working of a particular aspect of the life of the organisation. The average application programmer in contrast will have far more technical knowledge than enterprise knowledge.

The two other roles on the graph have emerged with the rise of the database concept. In many organisations the roles of data administrator and database administrator are frequently confused. We make the distinction here between a database administrator who normally takes a low-level technical role of administering a particular company DBMS and database and a data administrator who tends to take a high-level, corporate-wide role of managing the data requirements of a particular organisation.

1.6 A Brief History of Database Software

The history of database software dates back to the early 1960s when the first data management systems were developed by individual companies to solve particular company problems. In the mid 1960s the first general purpose database packages became available. Perhaps the most famous of such packages was developed by the General Electric Company (GEC) called the Integrated Data Store (IDS), originally designed to run specifically on GEC machines. This package was largely the work of Charles Bachman.

B.F. Goodrich saw the work that was being done at GEC and decided to port IDS across onto the new IBM system 360 range of computers. John Cullinane entered into a marketing agreement with Goodrich. This was the beginning of a company named Cullinane, later Cullinet, which established the IDMS DBMS as the dominant force of network DBMS on IBM mainframes in the 1960s, 1970s and 1980s.

In 1969 a technical group operating under the auspices of CODASYL (Conference on Data Systems Languages) produced a specification of common database facilities which was strongly influenced by IDS and IDMS. The CODASYL model has been enhanced over the years to standardise the facilities of a range of DBMS.

In 1970 an IBM scientist Dr. E.F. Codd published an influential paper on database architecture entitled '*A Relational Model for Large Shared Data Banks*' (Codd, 1970). Researchers at IBM used the material in Codd's early publications to build the first prototype relational DBMS called System/R. This was emulated at a number of academic institutions, perhaps the foremost example being the INGRES research team at the University of Berkeley, California (Stonebraker, 1986).

During the 1970s and early 1980s relational databases got their primary support from academic establishments. The commercial arena was still dominated by IDMS-type databases. In 1983, however, IBM announced its first relational database for large mainframes - DB2. Since that time, relational databases have grown from strength to strength.

1.7 Data Models

Database work has always been strong in terms of practice. It is only with the rise of relational database systems however that database work has been given a strong theoretical underpinning. When people talk of the theory of databases they are normally referring to data models. It is to this concept that we now turn.

1.7.1 The Two Meanings

The term data model, like many other terms in computing, is somewhat ambiguous. In the literature the term is used in at least two senses. In the first sense, the sense to which we shall devote most attention, the term data model is used to describe an architecture for data. In the second sense, the sense we shall examine mainly in chapter 7, the term is used to describe the rules of some business application.

At this point, we can make a direct analogy with building. The architecture of building is made up of some set of principles involved in determining how a building can be built from a set of component materials to some predetermined style. An architecture of building consists of a set of components and techniques.

An architecture of data is similar in conception. The component materials are more abstract than the bricks and mortar of an architecture of building, but an architect of data still has to have some conception of how to build a database from underlying data structures.

In the second sense, the term data model is analogous to a completed building or perhaps more accurately to the design for a building. In an architectural design, the building architect will have applied some principles of architecture to satisfy the demands or requirements of his client. In a database design, the data architect will have modelled the rules of some enterprise, the requirements of his client, by applying the concepts of his data architecture.

1.7.2 Relational Data Model

Any data model, in the architectural sense, is generally held to consist of three components (Tsitchizris, 1982):

(1)   a set of data structures
(2)   a set of data operators
(3)   a set of inherent integrity rules.

These three components are frequently referred to as data definition, data manipulation and data integrity respectively. To these we add a fourth component, data control - a set of database control functions - which is extremely important to modern database management.

The Relational Data Model is intrinsically simple. This is its primary appeal. As the American architect Mies Van Der Rohe once said '*Less is More*'. There is only one data structure in the Relational Data Model - the disciplined table or Relation. The operators of the model all act on such tables to produce new tables. The operators are bundled together in a set known as the Relational Algebra. There are also only two inherent integrity rules in the relational data model. One is known as Entity Integrity, the other as Referential Integrity.

To summarise, the Relational Data Model is made up of one data structure, eight fundamental operators and two inherent integrity rules. To this we add a concern with controlling access to a database via the concept of a view.

1.8 The SQL Standard

In this work we will continually reflect the relational data model against the contemporary practice of relational database systems. Contemporary practice is primarily centred around a database language known as SQL (Structured Query Language).

SQL has its origins in work done at the IBM research laboratory in San Jose, California in the early 1970s. Here the prototype implementation of relational concepts named System/R was built. This early RDBMS embodied a language then known as SEQUEL. Many people still refer to the SQL language by this term rather than the acronym. Because of the success of the initial prototype IBM made the decision to develop a

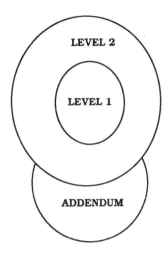

Figure 1.6

range of of products founded on relational technology: SQL/DS, QMF and more recently DB2.

During the years 1973 to 1979 IBM researchers published a great deal of material about the development of System/R in academic journals. This period was characterised by intense discussion about the validity of RDBMS at conferences and seminars both in the US and in Europe. IBM however was undoubtedly slow to see the commercial relevance of relational systems. It fell to the ORACLE corporation, founded in 1977, to first exploit successfully in the commercial world the ideas underlying the relational data model.

ORACLE was, and is, an SQL-based RDBMS. Many other vendors have also produced systems that support SQL. For these reasons, in 1982 the American National Standards Committee gave its database committee (X3H2) the remit to develop a standard Relational Database Language (RDL). This committee finally produced a definition for a standard SQL syntax in 1986 primarily based on the IBM dialect of SQL (ANSI, 1986). The International Standards Organisation followed suit with a publication of much the same standard in 1987 (ISO, 1987). The original ANSI document specifies two levels for SQL: level one and level two. Level two is the complete SQL language. Level one is a subset of level two originally intended to act as the intersection of existing implementations (see figure 1.6).

Following its publication, a number of criticisms were made of the ANSI/ISO standard, most notably by database personalities such as E.F. Codd and C. Date (see chapter 8). Many people viewed the standard as suffering from being the lowest common denominator amongst implementations. Others saw the language to have more serious defects particularly in its ability to address relational constructs.

In response to some of these criticisms, an addendum to the standard was published in 1989 by ANSI primarily addressing a number of integrity enhancement features (ANSI, 1989a). Much of the material in this addendum was included in a working draft of a proposed second version to the standard also published by ANSI in 1989 (ANSI, 1989b). ISO, working in close collaboration with ANSI, published a document in the same year entitled 'Database Language SQL with Integrity Enhancement' (ISO, 1989).

Both the ANSI and ISO documents represent currently incomplete specifications for a major revision to the standards to be known as SQL2. A complete specification for SQL2 is expected sometime in 1991. Further substantial enhancements to the SQL2 standard have however already been agreed, and a version known as SQL3 is to be expected sometime in the mid-1990s. Figure 1.7 summarises the derivation of the present standards.

Most vendor implementations of SQL differ in some way from the standard. Vendor implementations are more accurately seen as dialects of the SQL standard. In other words, they find common ground in many respects usually formulated around some definition of the core or level one of the standard. In other respects they differ by not adhering to the standard in certain areas (data types is a good example) or they offer facilities not included in the standard.

ORACLE's version SQL*plus is deficient in some respects and strong in others. ORACLE is accurately portrayed as a robust implementation of the ANSI standard for SQL (ANSI, 1986). It also offers additional facilities which are particularly suitable for application building (see chapter 7). The version of SQL supplied by ORACLE however does not offer in an active way any of the integrity enhancement features expected for SQL2.

The standard is therefore a moving and somewhat mystical entity. When anybody talks of the SQL standard at database conferences, for instance, the cry is frequently one of, *'Which standard?'* Whatever your view

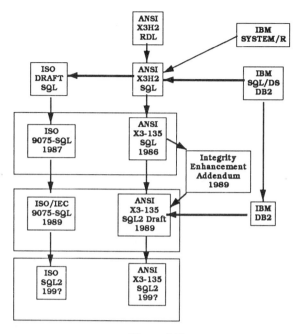

Figure 1.7

of SQL however, because of activities centred around the standards-making bodies, this particular database language will be in use for a long time yet. SQL looks like becoming the glue not only between database products but also between database systems and Computer Aided Software Engineering (CASE) tools. Some knowledge of SQL is therefore a must for any developer of information systems in the short- and medium-term future (Beynon-Davies, 1989) (see chapter 7).

1.9 Conclusion

In this chapter we have set the scene for the discussion which follows. We began by examining some of the problems which led to the development of database systems. This was followed by an introduction to the characteristics of databases, DBMS and data models, particularly the Relational Data Model. We then provided a brief history of the development of database software and concluded by examining the place that the SQL standard is playing in the database arena.

The next four chapters discuss in some detail the four data modelling aspects of data definition, data manipulation, data integrity and data control and reflect these against their implementation in the database language SQL.

1.10 Exercises

(1)   What are the primary properties of a database system?

(2)   Why did we describe a database system as being analogous to a series of filing cabinets?

(3)   What are the facilities you would expect to find in a DBMS?

(4)   Define the difference between an architectural data model and a business data model.

(5)   What are the primary components of a data model?

(6)   Define the Relational Data Model in terms of the standard components of a data model.

(7)   What benefits arise from having a standard interface to RDBMS?

Chapter 2
Data Definition

2.1 What is Data Definition?

A database is effectively a set of data structures for organising and storing data. In any data model, and consequently in any DBMS, we must have a set of principles for exploiting such data structures for business applications. Data definition is the process of exploiting the inherent data structures of a data model for a particular business application.

2.2 The Data Model

In this chapter we first consider the single data structure inherent to the Relational Data Model. We also consider a set of principles for organising business data using this data structure centred around the concepts of a primary and foreign key.

2.2.1 Codd's Objectives

In developing the Relational Data Model E.F.Codd claims to have adhered to a dictum of Albert Einstein, 'make it as simple as possible, but no simpler'. The last point of the dictum discourages the pursuit of simplicity if it distorts reality (Codd, 1990).

From 1968 to 1988 Codd published more than 30 technical papers on the Relational Data Model. He refers to the total content of the pre-1979 papers as version one of the Relational Data Model (Codd, 1990).

Early in 1979, Codd presented a paper to the Australian Computer Society at Hobart, Tasmania entitled 'Extending the Relational Database Model to Capture More Meaning'. The paper was later to be published in the ACM Database Transactions (Codd, 1979). The extended version of the Relational Data Model discussed in this paper Codd named RM/T (T for Tasmania).

Early in 1990 Codd published a book entitled 'The Relational Model for Database Management: Version 2' (Codd, 1990). One of the main reasons Codd cites for publishing this work is that he believes that many vendors of DBMS products with the relational stamp have failed to understand the implications not only of RM/T but also many aspects of version one of the model.

Codd has always maintained that there were three problems that he wanted to address with his theoretical work:

(1)   he wanted to directly enhance the concept of program - data independence.

(2)   he maintained that prior data models treated data in an undisciplined fashion. His model was proposed as a disciplined way of handling data using the rigour of mathematics.

(3)   he wanted to improve programmer productivity. In 1982, when Codd received the ACM Turing award, the title of his acceptance paper was, '*Relational Database: a Practical Foundation for Productivity*' (Codd, 1982).

2.2.2 One Data Structure

One of the major attractions of the Relational Data Model is its simplicity. It is simple because it has only one data structure - the disciplined table or relation.

When Codd embarked on his early work, his intent was to be precise, rigorous and unambiguous. Being a mathematician Codd naturally turned to mathematics, particularly a branch of mathematics known as set theory, to supply these characteristics. The Relational Data Model is therefore peppered with terms from mathematics.

(1)   Tables are referred to as relations

(2)   Rows are called tuples

(3)   Columns are called attributes

(4)   The number of columns in a relation is said to be the degree of the relation

(5)   The number of rows in a relation is said to be the cardinality of the relation.

Even Codd however has relaxed his use of the strict terminology of the data model. He frequently talks of tables, rows and columns rather than relations, tuples and attributes. We shall follow suit in this work as long as the reader is aware of some subtleties to which we now turn.

2.2.3 Relations Vs Tables

Although the structure below is a table in common parlance, to Codd it is a Relation. A Relation is a disciplined table. A table which obeys a certain restricted set of rules.

DEPARTMENTS

Deptno	Dname	Location
10	Accounting	London
20	Research	Bristol
30	Sales	London
40	Operations	Birmingham

(1) Every relation in a database must have a distinct name. A two-dimensional table for Codd is a mathematical set. Mathematical sets must be named unambiguously.

(2) Every column in a relation must have a distinct name within the relation. Each column of a relation is also a set and hence should also be named unambiguously.

(3) All entries in a column must be of the same kind.

(4) The ordering of columns in a relation is not significant. The head of a relation - its list of column names - is also a mathematical set. Sets in mathematics are not ordered.

(5) Each row in a relation must be distinct. In other words, duplicate rows are not allowed in a relation.

(6) The ordering of rows is not significant. There should be no implied order in the storage of rows in a relation. The body of a relation is a set.

(7) Each cell or column/row intersection in a relation should contain only a so-called atomic value. In other words, multi-values are not allowed in a relation.

These rules characterise relations as a subset of what we normally understand by the general term table (see figure 2.1).

DATA STRUCTURE = RELATION

A Relation is a disciplined table

All columns must have unique names
All column entries must be of same kind
The ordering of columns is not significant
Each row must be distinct
Each column/row intersection should contain a single value
Ordering of rows is not significant
Every relation must have a primary key

PRODUCTS		
product	*product*	*product*
number	*name*	*price*
485	widget	1.0
289	woggle	2.0
333	wangle	0.5

Figure 2.1

2.2.4 Primary Keys

To enforce the property of a relation that duplicate rows are forbidden each relation must have a so-called primary key. A primary key is one or more columns of a table whose values are used to uniquely identify each of the rows in a table.

In any relation there may be a number of candidate keys. That is, a column or group of columns which can act in the capacity of a unique identifier. The primary key is chosen from one of the candidate keys.

Consider, for instance, the relation on the next page.

Empno, ename and *hiredate* are currently candidate keys. We know in practice, of course, that as the size of the employees file grows we are likely to store information about more than one employee named *Smith*, and more than one employee is likely to be hired on the same day. This leaves *empno* - a unique code for each employee - as the only practicable primary key.

EMPLOYEES

Empno	Ename	Job	Mgr	Hiredate	Salary	Comm	Deptno
7369	Smith	Clerk	7902	17-DEC-80	800		20
7499	Allen	Salesman	7698	20-FEB-81	1600	300	30
7521	Ward	Salesman	7698	22-FEB-81	1250	300	30
7566	Jones	Manager	7839	02-APR-81	2975		20
7654	Martin	Salesman	7698	28-SEP-81	1250		30
7698	Blake	Manager	7839	01-MAY-81	2850		30
7782	Clarke	Manager	7839	09-JUN-81	2450		10
7788	Scott	Analyst	7566	09-NOV-81	3000		20
7839	King	President		17-NOV-81	5000		10
7844	Turner	Salesman	7698	08-SEP-81	1500	0	30
7876	Adams	Clerk	7788	23-SEP-81	1100		20
7900	James	Clerk	7698	03-DEC-81	950		30
7902	Ford	Analyst	7566	02-DEC-81	3000		20
7934	Miller	Clerk	7782	23-JAN-82	1300		10

In the *departments* table discussed earlier in section 2.2.3, *deptno* and *dname* are candidate keys. *Deptno* is probably however the logical choice for a primary key for reasons to be discussed in the next section.

Any candidate key, and consequently any primary key, must have two properties. It must be unique, and it must not be null. First, by definition any candidate key must be a unique identifier. Hence, there can be no duplicate values in a candidate or primary key column. Second, we must have a primary key value for each row in a table. In other words, we cannot have a null (non-existent) value within a primary key column or columns.

2.2.5 Object Identifiers

To reiterate, primary keys are an essential component of the relational data model. Every table in a relational database must have a primary key. But how do you choose a primary key? The present section presents a number of guidelines based around a series of properties that a primary key should have. The first two properties we have already discussed:

(1) The primary key must be unique for every instance of an object in the database. Every fact in a database must be unequivocally identifiable via the primary key.

(2) The primary key must have a definite value for every instance of an object. We must not allow a null value for the primary key.

These first two properties are structural in the sense that they define what it means to be a primary key - an attribute that is unique and not null.

(3) A primary key value must be made explicit immediately an instance of an object is created. Consider the case where a company receives an order from a new customer. The sales person taking the order may be tempted to take information about the customer such as his name and address without assigning him an identifier. This must be forbidden if we are to ensure the integrity of the orders database.

(4) Every instance of an object should be associated with one and only one value of a primary key. We should not have several records in our products file each describing the same product instance but using different primary key values. Occasionally, there is a requirement to trace a particular object over time or across organisational boundaries. If an instance of a product appears in various guises in our system, there is no consistent way of tracing the object over time or throughout our organisation.

(5) The primary key should not contain details about the properties of the object it is representing. A primary key should do nothing more than uniquely identify an object. In this capacity it can remain relatively stable. If it represents some property of the object such as its name then the primary key is potentially unstable. Properties of objects are likely to change over time.

Consider the case of a company which uses 3-digit number to identify its products. The first digit represents the warehouse at which the product is stored.This situation works well if the company practices remain relatively unchanged. If a company decision is made to re-site widgets at another warehouse however then all occurrences of this product code must be changed in the database.

(6) We should be able to maintain control over primary key values. Unless we have complete control over the assignment of primary key values we cannot ensure that they will remain unique. We should therefore resist the temptation to use primary key data supplied by outside agencies. Consider the case of a company which uses a delivery advice number as a primary key to its delivery advices file. This number is taken off the advice note sent by suppliers. Such a situation is open to a number of problems. A given supplier may inadvertently, for instance, send two advices having the same number.

(7) The primary key must be known to end-users. Some people argue that the primary key should act in the capacity of a surrogate identifier. In other words, it should be a system-generated identifier transparent to the user. The argument is that the user should access data using more natural properties of objects such as names, job titles etc. However a primary key is undoubtedly the only consistent, direct mechanism for locating an object in a database. It is therefore essential that the user be given the opportunity to access data using this mechanism.

The consequence of the seven properties detailed above is that the best

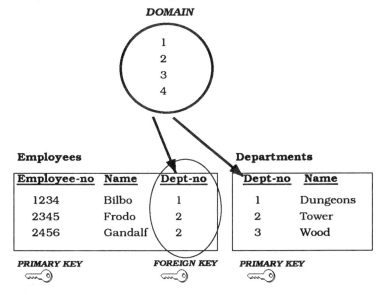

Figure 2.2

candidate for a primary key is a unique serial number having no mnemonic capacity. *Empno* in the *employees* table is a unique serial number, as is *deptno* in the *departments* table. Both columns act merely as a reference and tell us nothing about employees or departments.

2.2.6 One Access Method

Primary keys are of fundamental importance to the Relational Data Model. This is because, in combination with the table or relation name, a primary key value provides the sole addressing mechanism in the Relational Data Model. In other words, the only guaranteed way of locating a given row from a database is via a combination of table name and primary key value. This is the reason that the Relational Data Model is often referred to as a value-oriented data model (Ullman, 1989).

For example, the only way we can uniquely locate properties of the person object named 'Allen' from our employees table is via a combination of the table name *employees* and the *empno 7499* (see the table in section 2.2.4).

2.2.7 Domains

The primary unit of data in the Relational Data Model is the data item, for example, a part number, a customer number or a person's date of birth. Such data items are said to be non-decomposable or atomic. A set of such data items of the same type is said to be a domain. For example, the domain of customer numbers is the set of all possible customer numbers. Domains are therefore pools of values from which actual values appearing in the columns of a table are drawn.

According to Codd, the concept of a domain has played a very important role in the development of the Relational Data Model. One reason for this is that if two columns draw their values from the same domain then comparisons (particularly an operation known as the join to be discussed in chapter 3) between these columns make sense. Hence a comparison between the *deptno* column of the *employees* table and the *deptno* column in the *departments* table has some validity. In contrast, a comparison between employee names and department names does not make sense. We may have an employee with the surname *London*, but people are different objects from departments. They draw their values from different domains (see figure 2.2).

Theoreticians like Codd and Date make a cogent argument for a DBMS mechanism which would allow the explicit declaration of domains (Codd, 1990). One of the main advantages of such a mechanism is that it is important in supporting a number of data integrity issues (see chapter 4). At the time of writing, no vendor of RDBMS supports a domain definition mechanism with sufficient functionality to satisfy Codd and Date.

2.2.8 Foreign Keys

Foreign keys are the glue of relational systems. They are the means of interconnecting the information stored in a series of disparate tables.

A foreign key is a column or group of columns of some table which draws its values from the same domain as the primary key of some other table in the database. In our personnel example *deptno* is a foreign key in the *employees* table. This column draws its values from the same domain as the *deptno* column - the primary key of the *departments* table. This means that when we know the *deptno* of some employee we can cross-refer to the *departments* table to see where that employee is located. Figure 2.3

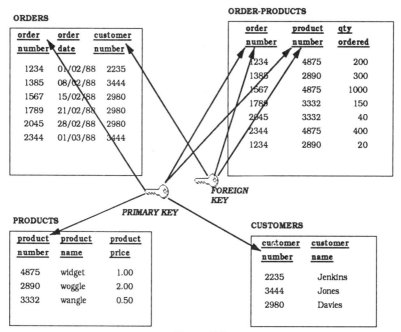

Figure 2.3

illustrates the use of foreign keys in a database of four tables.

2.2.9 The System Catalog

In order for a Relational DBMS to work effectively, such a DBMS must be able to access information about the structure of a particular database. The place where such information is stored is referred to by various names - system catalog, the system tables, data dictionary - are just three.

In a relational system the system catalog is a database conforming to the same data structure conventions as a normal database. The system catalog is frequently referred to as a meta-database. Meta means *over or above*. The system catalog is therefore a set of tables storing higher-level information about the underlying structure of the base tables.

The core information that must be stored in the catalog comprises a description of each base relation in terms of relation names, column names, column data types or domains and primary key references. Other information such as foreign key references, index and view information is also appropriate.

Since a system catalog is simply a set of tables we would expect the same maintenance operations that apply to base tables to apply to system tables as well. In practice, only querying system tables works in the same manner as base tables. Most users of the database system are prohibited from accessing the system tables directly for insert, update or delete operations. Such operations are normally executed via specific data definition commands most of which are normally only provided for use by the database administrator. It is to the way in which SQL addresses such issues that we now turn.

2.3 The DBMS

The second half of this chapter is devoted to considering how the Data Definition Language (DDL) of SQL operates. We specifically consider the DDL of the ISO 87 standard (ISO, 1987) and ORACLE's dialect SQL*Plus. We discuss how to create and modify tables, how to create indexes and how to delete tables and indexes. Because of the importance of the concept, we also discuss a create domain command as proposed in a new standard for SQL (ISO, 1989).

2.3.1 *The CREATE TABLE Statement*

To form a table using SQL we need to know four things:

(1) the name of the table
(2) the name of each of the columns in the table
(3) the data type of each column
(4) the maximum length of each column.

These four items are formulated together in a CREATE TABLE command:

```
CREATE TABLE <table name>
        (<column name> <data type> (<length>),
        <column name> <data type> (<length>),
        ..              ..          ..      )
```

The statement below, for instance, demonstrates how the *employees* table might be created.

```
CREATE TABLE employees
        (empno NUMBER(4),
        ename CHAR(10),
        job CHAR(9),
        mgr NUMBER(4),
        hiredate DATE,
        salary NUMBER(7,2),
        comm NUMBER(7,2),
        deptno NUMBER(2))
```

Note the following points about the above definition.

(i) The DATE data type does not need a length since dates are stored in a standard internal format

(ii) The NUMBER data type can either represent an integer, as in NUMBER(2), or a decimal, as in NUMBER(7,2). The digit after the comma represents the number of digits after the decimal point.

2.3.2 Data Types

The *char, number* and *date* data types act in part as a definition for domains. Data types define certain properties about the allowable values for a column. Every data value within a column must be of the same type. The SQL standard (ISO, 1987) defines some eight data types: *character, decimal, smallint, real, numeric, integer, float,* and *double precision.* The ORACLE dialect permits just four: *char, number, date* and *long.*

> **Char**. Columns of this type contain strings of characters of a given maximum length.
> **Number**. Columns of this type contain numbers with an optional sign and number of digits after the decimal point.
> **Date**. The standard format for dates is DD-MON-YY as in 05-MAR-57. Dates can however be turned into character strings and manipulated in various ways.
> **Long**. Columns of this type can contain text up to a system-defined maximum length.

In most practical situations only the first three data types are used.

2.3.3 A Proposed CREATE DOMAIN Command

In the ISO 1987 standard there is no straightforward way of declaring the domain of a particular column or columns. In the proposed draft standard for SQL2 (ISO, 1989) however a CREATE DOMAIN command is specified. Because of the importance of the concept we illustrate the use of this command in this section.

Suppose, for instance we wish to declare a domain for the *job* column of the *employees* table. Let us assume that we have job specifications only for the following list of jobs in our company: *Clerk, Salesman, Analyst, Manager, President*. This defines then the pool of values comprising our domain. We declare this domain with the following statement:

```
CREATE DOMAIN jobd AS CHAR(10)
CHECK (job IN
('Clerk', 'Salesman', 'Analyst', 'Manager', 'President'))
```

In the create table statement we can now use this domain to reference the appropriate column.

```
CREATE TABLE employees
    (empno NUMBER(4),
    ename CHAR(10),
    job DOMAIN jobd,
    mgr NUMBER(4),
    hiredate DATE,
    salary NUMBER(7,2),
    comm NUMBER(7,2),
    deptno NUMBER(2))
```

This is a far more effective mechanism than a straightforward data type declaration since it includes an added integrity check. Users will now be prohibited from entering any values outside the prescribed pool of values for the *job* column. Data integrity will be discussed in more detail in chapter 4.

2.3.4 The CREATE INDEX Statement

In Codd's early papers on the Relational Data Model little attention was paid to questions of performance, particularly retrieval performance. In any relational database system however the question of how long it takes to gain a response to a query is of fundamental importance.

The main way of achieving performance advantages in SQL-based systems is by adding indexes to the database. Conceptually, an index is a table made up of two columns. One column stores the data values that we wish to retrieve. The other column stores a series of pointers to the rows in a table (see figure 2.4).

To build an index in SQL we use the CREATE INDEX statement:

```
CREATE INDEX <index name>
ON <table name> (<column name>)
```

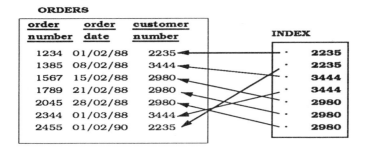

Figure 2.4

For example,

    CREATE INDEX emp_ind
    ON employees(empno)

2.3.5 Declaring Primary Keys

There is no direct mechanism for declaring primary keys either in the core
SQL standard (ISO, 1987) or in ORACLE's dialect of SQL, SQL*Plus. An
addendum to the standard does however propose a direct mechanism,
and IBM's latest relational product - DB2 - does have a facility for declaring
primary keys directly. These issues will be left to chapter 4. In this section
we shall discuss the indirect mechanisms available in most contemporary
RDBMS.

In section 2.2.4 we discussed the two properties of a primary key as
being an attribute which is unique and not null. We can assign the not null
characteristic to a column by adding a keyword to a table definition as
below.

    CREATE TABLE employees
        (empno NUMBER(4) NOT NULL,
        ename CHAR(10),
        job CHAR(9),
        mgr NUMBER(4),
        hiredate DATE,

```
        salary NUMBER(7,2),
        comm NUMBER(7,2),
        deptno NUMBER(2))
```

Some RDBMS also allow the addition of a UNIQUE keyword to enforce the uniqueness characteristic.

```
    CREATE TABLE employees
        (empno NUMBER(4) NOT NULL UNIQUE,
        ename CHAR(10),
        job CHAR(9),
        mgr NUMBER(4),
        hiredate DATE,
        salary NUMBER(7,2),
        comm NUMBER(7,2),
        deptno NUMBER(2))
```

In ORACLE, uniqueness has to be enforced by creating a UNIQUE index on a column.

```
    CREATE UNIQUE INDEX emp_ind
    ON employees(empno)
```

2.3.6 Declaring Foreign Keys

There is no way of declaring foreign keys in most contemporary RDBMS. DB2 is an exception and is discussed in chapter 4. This issue is a fast developing area in RDBMS and we are likely to see a lot of progress over the next few years.

The notion of a foreign key and the integrity issues it raises are normally addressed within conventional information systems work via application programs sitting atop a database. In chapter 7, for instance, we shall discuss how to address this issue using ORACLE's application builder SQL*Forms.

2.3.7 The System Tables

Every time a table or index definition is issued to the DBMS, entries are made in a number of system tables. The set of system tables is not defined in the standard. It is product-specific. ORACLE, for instance, maintains some 43 system tables. A sample from this meta-database is presented below (ORACLE, 1987b).

Catalog   Tables and views accessible to the user excluding the system tables
Columns   Columns in tables accessible to the userexcluding the system tables
Col   Specifications of columns in tables created by the user
Indexes   Indexes created by the user and indexes on   tables created by the user

2.3.8 DROP TABLE and DROP INDEX

Table definitions can be created and table definitions can be deleted. To remove a table from the database we use the following command:

    DROP TABLE <table name>

For example,

    DROP TABLE employees

One must be careful using this command as many RDBMS such as ORACLE do not issue any warning to the user.

One of the main strengths of relational databases is that indexes can be created and deleted with relative abandon. To delete an index we use the following command:

    DROP INDEX <index name>

For example,

    DROP INDEX emp_ind

2.3.9 Modifying Tables

To reiterate some of the discussion of chapter 1, the ideal of data independence dictates that a database administrator should be allowed to modify the structure of a database without impacting on the users or application programs which access this database. In practice, SQL-based products support only a limited form of data-independence. The database administrator is allowed to add an extra column to a table or modify the maximum length of an existing column. Both operations are specified using the ALTER TABLE command.

> ALTER TABLE <table name>
> [ADD : MODIFY] (<column name> <data type> <length>)

For instance,

> ALTER TABLE employees
> ADD (marital_status char(1))
>
> ALTER TABLE employees
> MODIFY (job char(20))

2.4 Conclusion

In this chapter we began by considering Codd's objectives for developing the relational data model. In essence, his aim was to develop a simple but rigorous approach to data management. This simplicity is evident in the relational data model's approach to data structures. We discussed in some detail the one data structure of the relational data model. This led to a consideration of the related concepts of primary key, foreign key and domain.

In part two we considered how ISO standard SQL implements Codd's ideas on data definition. Our aim has been to emphasise some of the disparities between the model as proposed and its implementation in the database sub-language SQL and existing relational products.

Data definition is the process of declaring a structure for data. To make a useful database system however we must also have mechanisms for inserting data into the database, amending the data already in our database, and, most importantly, making enquiries of the data stored in our database. It is to this topic of data manipulation that we turn next.

2.5 Exercises

(1)   Why is a relation described as being a disciplined table?

(2)   Why is the table below not a relation?

Ward Name	Ward Type	No of Beds	Sister	Patient No.	Patient Name	Date of Birth
Bryn Siriol	Paediatric	6	N Hughes	3424	J Beynon	05-JAN-87
				2567	T Jones	10-MAR-88
				6789	R Burton	21-APR-89
Cefn Coed	Geriatric	8	T Evans	4545	P Davies	05-MAR-05
				3434	G Evans	10-OCT-10
Merthyr	General	10	M Thomas	2344	R Coles	10-JUN-67

(3)   Define what is meant by the term primary key.

(4)   Define what is meant by the term foreign key.

(5)   Define what is meant by the term domain.

(6)   What type of data item is best suited to act as a primary key?

(7)   What role do the system tables fulfil in relational systems?

(8)   Define the structure of the *departments* table using an SQL CREATE TABLE statement.

(9)   Declare deptno to be the primary key of the table using SQL.

(10)   Change the size of the loc column of the *departments* table to 20 characters.

(11)   Create an index on the location column of the *departments* table.

(12)   Delete the location index.

(13)   Delete the *departments* table from the database.

(14)   Which varies more, the cardinality of a relation or the degree of a relation?

Chapter 3
Data Manipulation

3.1 What is Data Manipulation?

In the last chapter we considered the data definition part of the relational model. In this chapter we discuss the second of the three parts of the relational data model: that part dealing with data manipulation.

Data manipulation has four aspects:

(1) How we input data into a relation
(2) How we remove data from a relation
(3) How we amend data in a relation
(4) How we retrieve data from a relation.

When Codd first proposed the relational data model by far the most attention was devoted to the final aspect of data manipulation - information retrieval. That is, how we run queries on our database and extract information to satisfy these queries. It is only relatively recently in his publications on version 2 of the data model that Codd has devoted considerable attention to the other three conventional aspects of data manipulation (Codd, 1990).

3.2 The Data Model

Because of its importance, we devote most of the attention to information retrieval in this chapter. We begin with a detailed discussion of Codd's original proposals for the operators of the relational model - the relational algebra. We then cast the operators of this abstract machine in terms of information retrieval under the SQL standard. Finally, we consider how SQL handles the file maintenance operations of insertion, update, and deletion.

3.2.1 Why the Relational Algebra?

In his early papers, Codd proposed a collection of operators for manipulating relations (Codd, 1970). He called the entire collection of such

operators the relational algebra. Codd's intention was to demonstrate a theoretical retrieval language which operates on entire
relations and produced relations as results. However, few actual contemporary relational DBMS use the relational algebra for information retrieval. The question then is, why bother to study a retrieval language
which is primarily abstract?

The main reason is that the relational algebra is the fundamental
basis of languages like SQL. The operators of the algebra are primitives out of which actual relational query languages have been built.

Another reason is that an understanding of the relational algebra is
essential for understanding numerous other aspects of relational systems
eg, query optimisation, database design, database distribution etc.

3.2.2 What is the Relational Algebra?

The relational algebra is a set of some eight operators. Each operator takes
one or more relations as input and produces one relation as output. The
three main operators of the algebra are *select, project* and *join.* Using these
three operators most of the manipulation required of relational systems
can be accomplished.

The additional operators - *product, union, intersection, difference* and

Relational   **Manipulative Part Of**
Algebra   =   **Relational Model**

ALGEBRAIC OPERATORS ACT ON
WHOLE RELATIONS

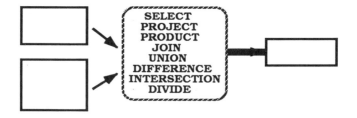

Figure 3.1

division - are modelled on the traditional operators of set theory. Figure 3.1 summarises this discussion.

3.2.3 The Personnel Database

To demonstrate the power of the relational algebra, and later the informa- tion retrieval facilities of SQL, we shall use the small personnel database introduced in the previous chapter. This two-table database is based upon a subset of the demonstration system supplied with every ORACLE DBMS.

EMPLOYEES

Empno	Ename	Job	Mgr	Hiredate	Salary	Comm	Deptno
7369	Smith	Clerk	7902	17-DEC-80	800		20
7499	Allen	Salesman	7698	20-FEB-81	1600	300	30
7521	Ward	Salesman	7698	22-FEB-81	1250	300	30
7566	Jones	Manager	7839	02-APR-81	2975		20
7654	Martin	Salesman	7698	28-SEP-81	1250		30
7698	Blake	Manager	7839	01-MAY-81	2850		30
7782	Clarke	Manager	7839	09-JUN-81	2450		10
7788	Scott	Analyst	7566	09-NOV-81	3000		20
7839	King	President		17-NOV-81	5000		10
7844	Turner	Salesman	7698	08-SEP-81	1500	0	30
7876	Adams	Clerk	7788	23-SEP-81	1100		20
7900	James	Clerk	7698	03-DEC-81	950		30
7902	Ford	Analyst	7566	02-DEC-81	3000		20
7934	Miller	Clerk	7782	23-JAN-82	1300		10

DEPARTMENTS

Deptno	Dname	Location
10	Accounting	London
20	Research	Bristol
30	Sales	London
40	Operations	Birmingham

3.2.4 Select/Restrict

The *select* or *restrict* operator of the relational algebra takes a single relation as input and produces a single relation as output. Select is a 'horizontal slicer'. It extracts rows from the input relation matching a given condition and passes them to the output relation (se figure 3.2).

Using the *select* operator, the degree of the input relation is the same as that of the output relation. The cardinality of the output relation is less than or equal to the cardinality of the input relation.

There is no standard syntax for the operators of the relational algebra. We therefore use here a syntax designed more for understandability than for rigour.

> SELECT <table name>
> [WHERE <condition>] -> <result table>

eg.,

> SELECT employees WHERE ename = 'Allen' -> T1

SELECT (restrict)

Create a subset of rows in a table according to a given condition

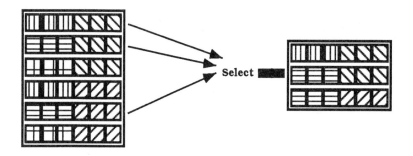

Figure 3.2

Result:

T1

Empno	Ename	Job	Mgr	Hiredate	Salary	Comm	Deptno
7499	Allen	Salesman	7698	20-FEB-81	1600	300	30

3.2.5 Project

The *project* operator takes a single relation as input and produces a single relation as output. *Project* is a 'vertical slicer'. The cardinality of the input relation is the same as the cardinality of the output relation. The degree of the output relation is less than or equal to the degree of the input relation (see figure 3.3).

The syntax for the project operator is as follows:

PROJECT <table name> [<column list>] -> <result table>

eg,

PROJECT departments(deptno, dname) ->T1

PROJECT
Create a subset of columns in a table

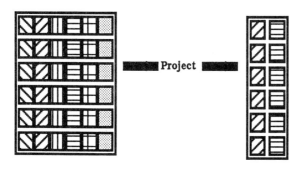

Project

Figure 3.3

Result:

T1

Deptno	Dname
10	Accounting
20	Research
30	Sales
40	Operations

3.2.6 Product

The relational operator *product* is a direct analogue of a set-theoretic operation known as the *Cartesian Product*. A *product* takes two relations as input and produces as output one relation composed of all the possible combinations of input tuples (see figure 3.4). The cardinality of the output relation is therefore equal to a multiplication of the cardinalities of the input relations. The degree of the output relation is equal to the addition of the degrees of the input relations. *Product* is a little-used operator in practice because of its potential for generating an 'information explosion'.

PRODUCT <table 1> WITH <table 2> -> <result   table>

eg,

PRODUCT employees WITH departments -> T1

Result:
T1

Empno	Ename	Job	Mgr	Hiredate	Salary	Comm	Deptno	Dname	Loc
7369	Smith	Clerk	7902	17-DEC-90	800		10	Accounting	London
7369	Smith	Clerk	7902	17-DEC-80	800		20	Research	Bristol
7369	Smith	Clerk	7902	17-DEC-80	800		30	Sales	London
7369	Smith	Clerk	7902	17-DEC-80	800		40	Operations	Birmingham
7499	Allen	Salesman	7698	20-FEB-81	1600	300	10	Accounting	London
7499	Allen	Salesman	7698	20-FEB-81	1600	300	20	Research	Bristol
7499	Allen	Salesman	7698	20-FEB-81	1600	300	30	Sales	London
7499	Allen	Salesman	7698	20-FEB-81	1600	300	40	Operations	Birmingham
7521	Ward	Salesman	7698	22-FEB-81	1250	300	10	Accounting	London
7521	Ward	Salesman	7698	22-FEB-81	1250	300	20	Research	Bristol
7521	Ward	Salesman	7698	22-FEB-81	1250	300	30	Sales	London
7521	Ward	Salesman	7698	22-FEB-81	1250	300	40	Operations	Birmingham
7566	Jones	Manager	7839	02-APR-81	2975		10	Accounting	London
7566	Jones	Manager	7839	02-APR-81	2975		20	Research	Bristol
7566	Jones	Manager	7839	02-APR-81	2975		30	Sales	London
7566	Jones	Manager	7839	02-APR-81	2975		40	Operations	Birmingham
7654	Martin	Salesman	7698	28-SEP-81	1250		10	Accounting	London
7654	Martin	Salesman	7698	28-SEP-81	1250		20	Research	Bristol
7654	Martin	Salesman	7698	28-SEP-81	1250		30	Sales	London
7654	Martin	Salesman	7698	28-SEP-81	1250		40	Operations	Birmingham
7698	Blake	Manager	7839	01-MAY-81	2850		10	Accounting	London
7698	Blake	Manager	7839	01-MAY-81	2850		20	Research	Bristol
7698	Blake	Manager	7839	01-MAY-81	2850		30	Sales	London
7698	Blake	Manager	7839	01-MAY-81	2850		40	Operations	Birmingham
7782	Clarke	Manager	7839	09-JUN-81	2450		10	Accounting	London
7782	Clarke	Manager	7839	09-JUN-81	2450		20	Research	Bristol
7782	Clarke	Manager	7839	09-JUN-81	2450		30	Sales	London
7782	Clarke	Manager	7839	09-JUN-81	2450		40	Operations	Birmingham
7788	Scott	Analyst	7566	09-NOV-81	3000		10	Accounting	London
7788	Scott	Analyst	7566	09-NOV-81	3000		20	Research	Bristol
7788	Scott	Analyst	7566	09-NOV-81	3000		30	Sales	London
7788	Scott	Analyst	7566	09-NOV-81	3000		40	Operations	Birmingham
7839	King	President		17-NOV-81	5000		10	Accounting	London
7839	King	President		17-NOV-81	5000		20	Research	Bristol
7839	King	President		17-NOV-81	5000		30	Sales	London
7839	King	President		17-NOV-81	5000		40	Operations	Birmingham

etc.

PRODUCT
'Multiply' 2 tables
Combine all tuples from 2 tables

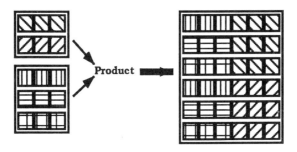

Figure 3.4

3.2.7 Join

The *join* operator takes two relations as input and produces one relation as output. A number of distinct types of *join* have been identified. Probably the most commonly used is the *natural join*, a development of the *equi-join*.

The *equi-join* operator is a *product* with an associated *select*. In other words, we combine two tables together but only for records matching a given condition (see figure 3,5).

    EQUIJOIN <table 1> WITH <table 2>
    ON <column name>
    WHERE <condition> - > <result table>

eg,

    EQUIJOIN employees WITH departments
    ON deptno
    WHERE job = 'Analyst' -> Tl

EQUI-JOIN

**Combine 2 tables on a common
column with restriction**

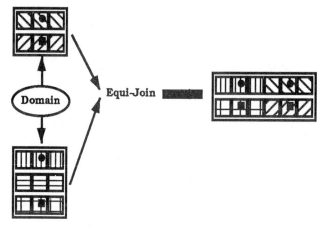

Figure 3.5

Result:

T1

Empno	Ename	Job	Mgr	Hiredate	Salary	Comm	Deptno	Deptno	Dname	Location
7788	Scott	Analyst	7566	09-NOV-81	3000		20	20	Research	Bristol
7902	Ford	Analyst	7566	02-DEC-81	3000		20	20	Research	Bristol

Note how the deptno column appears twice in the resulting table T1. An equi-join does not remove the duplicate join column. A *natural join* however does. The *natural join* or *join* operator is a *product* with an associated *select* followed by a *project* (see figure 3.6).

       JOIN <table 1> WITH <table 2>
       ON <column name>
       WHERE <condition> - > <result table>
eg,
       JOIN employees WITH departments
       ON deptno
       WHERE job = 'Analyst' -> T1

NATURAL JOIN

**Combine 2 tables on a common
column with restriction an projection**

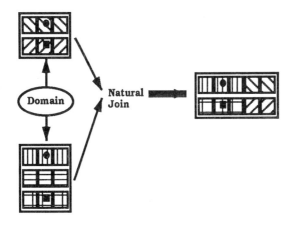

Figure 3.6

Result:

T1

Empno	Ename	Job	Mgr	Hiredate	Salary	Comm	Deptno	Dname	Location
7788	Scott	Analyst	7566	09-NOV-81	3000		20	Research	Bristol
7902	Ford	Analyst	7566	02-DEC-81	3000		20	Research	Bristol

3.2.8 A Procedural Query Language

The relational algebra is said to be a procedural query language. In other words, to extract information from a database using the algebra we have to specify a set of statements in some order. For example, consider the following query:

List the names and salaries of everybody in the research department

There are a number of ways we can implement this query using the algebra. Two possible solutions are given below:

SELECT departments WHERE dname = 'Research' -> T1
JOIN T1 WITH employees ON deptno -> T2
PROJECT T2(ename, salary) -> T3

JOIN departments WITH employees ON deptno -> T1
SELECT T1 WHERE dname = 'Research' -> T2
PROJECT T2(ename,salary) -> T

The relational algebra is a procedural query language because it demon-strates the property of closure. In other words, the output from the application of one relational operator can be passed as input to another relational operator, and so on. As we shall see in the second part of this chapter, some query languages, of which SQL is an example, do not demonstrate this property of closure.

3.2.9 Union

Union is an operator which takes two compatible relations as input and produces one relation as output. By compatible is meant that they have

UNION

Add 2 'union-compatible' tables together

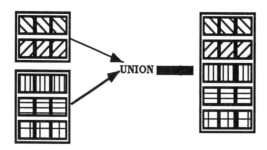

Figure 3.7

the same structure - the same columns defined on the same domains. Suppose, for instance, we segmented off manager and salesman records from our *employees* file into two seperate files, a *managers* file and a *salesmen* file. These two files could be reconstituted as one using the following command:

> UNION <table 1> WITH <table 2> -> <result table>
> UNION managers WITH salesmen -> T1

Result:

T1

Empno	Ename	Job	Mgr	Hiredate	Salary	Comm	Deptno
7499	Allen	Salesman	7698	20-FEB-81	1600	300	30
7521	Ward	Salesman	7698	22-FEB-81	1250	300	30
7566	Jones	Manager	7839	02-APR-81	2975		20
7654	Martin	Salesman	7698	28-SEP-81	1250		30
7698	Blake	Manager	7839	01-MAY-81	2850		30
7782	Clarke	Manager	7839	09-JUN-81	2450		10
7844	Turner	Salesman	7698	08-SEP-81	1500	0	30

Note that the illustration in figure 3.7 indicates some overlap between the two input relations in terms of the output relation. In the example given here of course there is no such overlap. The structure of the *employees* file forbids somebody to be both a manager and a salesman.

3.2.10 Intersection

Intersection is fundamentally the opposite of *union.* Whereas *union* produces the combination of two sets or tables, *intersection* produces a result table which contains rows common to both input tables.

> INTERSECT <table 1> WITH <table 2> -> <result table>

eg,

> INTERSECT salesmen WITH managers -> T1

Applying intersection to the managers and salesmen file described in the previous section would give us the empty relation as a result. In other words, no employee in our company is both a salesman and a manager. Figure 3.8 illustrates the intersection operator.

INTERSECTION

**Create a table of rows
common to 2 tables**

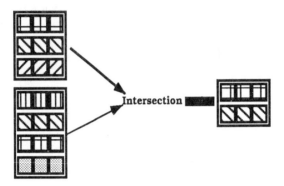

Figure 3.8

3.2.11 Difference

Whereas most operators in the relational algebra are commutative, *difference* or *minus* is not. In most operators, the order of specifying input relations is insignificant. A *union* of table 1 with table 2, for instance, is exacly the same as a *union* of table 2 with table 1. Using *difference*, in contrast, the order of specifying the input tables does matter. Hence,

DIFFERENCE salesmen WITH managers -> T1

will produce all salesmen who are not managers, while,

DIFFERENCE managers WITH salesmen -> T1

will produce all managers who are not salesmen (figure 3.9 demonstrates this).

3.2.12 Divide

The final operator we wish to discuss is *divide*. *Divide* takes two tables as

DIFFERENCE
'Subtract' 2 tables

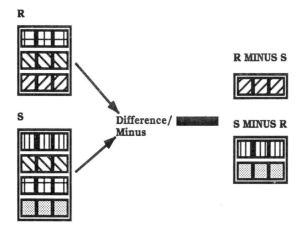

Figure 3.9

input and produces one table as output. One of the input tables must be a binary table, ie., it must have two columns. The other input table must be a unary table, ie., a one column table. The unary table must also be defined on the same domain as one of the columns of the binary table.

The fundamental idea of *divide* is that we take the values of the unary table and check them off against the compatible column from the binary table. Whenever all values from the unary table match with the same value from the binary table we output the value to the result table.

In figure 3.10 note how only the left-hand hatched cell is output. Only this cell matches with both the left upper circle and square of the unary table.

3.3 The DBMS

Although SQL has a data definition and file maintenance subset, the language was designed primarily as a means for extracting data from a database. Such extraction is accomplished through use of the *select*

DIVIDE

**Divide a table having 2 rows
by one having one row**

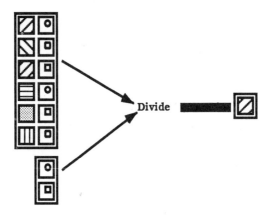

Figure 3.10

command: a combination of the *select, project,* and *join* operators of the
relational algebra.

3.3.1 Simple Retrieval

Simple retrieval is accomplished by a combination of the *select, from*
and *where* clauses:

> SELECT <attribute1 name>, <attribute2 name>, ...
> FROM <table name>
> [WHERE <condition>]

Select indicates the table columns to be retrieved. *From* defines the
tables to be referenced. *Where* indicates the condition to be satisfied.
The following command, for instance, is a direct analogue of the
relational algebra *select* or *restrict*. The asterisk - '*' - acts as a
wildcard. That is, all the attributes in the *employees* table are listed:

Query:

'List all the employee data'

Statement:

SELECT *
FROM employees

Result:

EMPLOYEES

Empno	Ename	Job	Mgr	Hiredate	Salary	Comm	Deptno
7369	Smith	Clerk	7902	17-DEC-80	800		20
7499	Allen	Salesman	7698	20-FEB-81	1600	300	30
7521	Ward	Salesman	7698	22-FEB-81	1250	300	30
7566	Jones	Manager	7839	02-APR-81	2975		20
7654	Martin	Salesman	7698	28-SEP-81	1250		30
7698	Blake	Manager	7839	01-MAY-81	2850		30
7782	Clarke	Manager	7839	09-JUN-81	2450		10
7788	Scott	Analyst	7566	09-NOV-81	3000		20
7839	King	President		17-NOV-81	5000		10
7844	Turner	Salesman	7698	08-SEP-81	1500	0	30
7876	Adams	Clerk	7788	23-SEP-81	1100		20
7900	James	Clerk	7698	03-DEC-81	950		30
7902	Ford	Analyst	7566	02-DEC-81	3000		20
7934	Miller	Clerk	7782	23-JAN-82	1300		10

Note that the example above has no *where* clause. The *where* clause is optional. If we omit the *where* clause then all the rows of a table are displayed. The addition of a *where* clause restricts the retrieval to a single row,

Query:

'List the record for Jones'

Statement:

SELECT *
FROM employees
WHERE Name = 'Jones';

Result:

Empno	Ename	Job	Mgr	Hiredate	Salary	Comm	Deptno
7566	Jones	Manager	7839	02-APR-81	2975		20

to a subset of the rows of a table,

Query:

'List all the employees in department 20'

Statement:

SELECT *
FROM employees
WHERE deptno = '20';

Result:

Empno	Ename	Job	Mgr	Hiredate	Salary	Comm	Deptno
7369	Smith	Clerk	7902	17-DEC-80	800		20
7566	Jones	Manager	7839	02-APR-81	2975		20
7788	Scott	Analyst	7566	09-NOV-81	3000		20
7876	Adams	Clerk	7788	23-SEP-81	1100		20
7902	Ford	Analyst	7566	02-DEC-81	3000		20

or even to a null set.

Query:

'List all the records for programmers'

Statement:

SELECT *
FROM employees
WHERE job = 'Programmer';

Result:

NO ROWS RETRIEVED

If we specify column names, then the SQL *select* becomes a combination of relational algebra *select* and *project*.

Query:

'List the employee numbers, names and jobs of all analysts'

Statement:

SELECT empno, name, job
FROM employees
WHERE job = 'Analyst';

Result:

Empno	Ename	Job
7788	Scott	Analyst
7902	Ford	Analyst

Query:

'List the jobs of employees hired after 1st November 1981'

Statement:

SELECT job
FROM emp
WHERE hiredate > '01-NOV-81';

Result:

Job

Analyst
President
Clerk
Analyst
Clerk

Note however, that since this table has duplicate values, it is not a relation. Duplicate values are legal in SQL, they are illegal as far as the relational data model is concerned. To produce a true relational response to the query above we must add the keyword *distinct* to the *select* clause. This removes duplicate entries in a table.

Statement:

SELECT DISTINCT job
FROM emp
WHERE hiredate > '01-NOV-81';

Result:

Job

Analyst
President
Clerk

3.3.2 Order By

In chapter 2 we discussed how there is no explicit ordering of rows in a relation. Ordering of data can therefore only be produced as a result of applying some processing to a relation. To produce a sorted list as output we add the *order by* clause to the *select* statement. For example,

Query:
> 'List all employee numbers, names, jobs and salaries of employees earning more than 2500 pounds per month in order of salary'

Statement:
> SELECT empno, name, job, salary
> FROM employees
> WHERE salary > 2500
> ORDER BY salary;

Result:

Empno	Ename	Job	Salary
7698	Blake	Manager	2850
7566	Jones	Manager	2975
7788	Scott	Analyst	3000
7902	Ford	Analyst	3000
7839	King	President	5000

The default order is ASCII ascending. To produce the list in descending order we add the keyword *desc*.

Query:
> 'List all employeee numbers, names, jobs and salaries of employees earning more than 2500 pounds per month in descending order of salary'

Statement:
> SELECT employee_no, name, job, salary
> FROM employees
> WHERE job = 'Analyst'
> ORDER BY salary DESC;

Result:

Empno	Ename	Job	Salary
7839	King	President	5000
7788	Scott	Analyst	3000
7902	Ford	Analyst	3000
7566	Jones	Manager	2975
7698	Blake	Manager	2850

3.3.3 Group By

To undertake aggregate work such as computing the average salary of employees in a particular department we use the *group by* clause:

Query:
'List the average salary and total number of persons in departments 10 and 20'

Statement:
SELECT deptno, avg(salary), count(*)
FROM employees
WHERE deptno IN (10,20)
GROUP BY deptno

Result:

Deptno	AVG(Salary)	COUNT(*)
10	2917	3
20	2175	5

Note the use of the *in* operator to specify a range of matchable values.

The following statement demonstrates the use of the HAVING clause:

Query:
'List all departments having more than 5 employees'

Statement:
SELECT deptno
FROM employees
GROUP BY deptno
HAVING count(*) > 5

Result:

 <u>**Deptno**</u>

 30

3.3.4 Aggregate Functions

Four functions are important for performing calculations on sets of data collated by a *group by* command: *max, min, avg,* and *count. Count,* for instance, returns the number of rows or values satisfying a query.

Query:

 'Count the number of employees'

Statement:

 SELECT count(*)
 FROM employees;

Result:

 14

Count can be used with *distinct* to tell us, for instance, how many job types are used in this company.

Query:

 'How many distinct job types are there in the employees file'

Statement:

 SELECT count(distinct job)
 FROM employees

Result:

 5

Max, min and *avg* are statistical functions which allow us to find the maximum, minimum and average of a set of values. We have already discussed *Avg;* here are two statements demonstrating the application of max and min.

Query:
'Find the maximum salary'

Statement:
SELECT max(salary)
FROM employees

Result:
5000

Query:
'Find the minimum commission'

Statement:
SELECT min(comm)
FROM employees

Result:
300

3.3.5 Subqueries

The word *structure* in Structured Query Language originally referred to the ability to nest queries in *select* statements. For instance, to find out who makes more money than Jones we would write:

Query:
'List the employee numbers and names of all persons who earn more than Jones'

Statement:
SELECTempno, name
FROM employees
WHERE salary >
   (SELECT salary
   FROM employees
   WHERE name = 'Jones');

Result:

Empno	Ename
7788	Scott
7839	King
7902	Ford

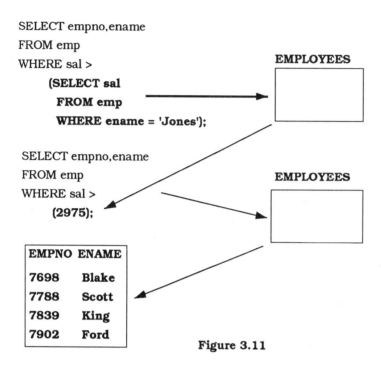

SELECT empno,ename
FROM emp
WHERE sal >
        (SELECT sal
            FROM emp
            WHERE ename = 'Jones');

SELECT empno,ename
FROM emp
WHERE sal >
        (2975);

EMPNO	ENAME
7698	Blake
7788	Scott
7839	King
7902	Ford

Figure 3.11

SQL evaluates the innermost query first. This produces a result which is compared with the result produced from the outermost query. Figure 3.11 illustrates this process.

Query:

'List the employee number, names and salaries of all persons in department 20 who earn more than anybody in department 30'

Statement:

SELECT ename
FROM employees
WHERE deptno = 20
        AND salary >
        (SELECT max(salary)
        FROM employees
        WHERE deptno = '30');

Result:

Empno	Name	Salary
7566	Jones	2975
7788	Scott	3000
7902	Ford	3000

3.3.6 Correlated Subqueries

In the previous two examples, the subquery was executed once. The resulting value was then used in the *where* clause of the outermost query. A subquery can however execute repeatedly. In this case it produces a series of values to be matched against the results of the outermost query. Consider, for instance, the following request:

List the employee name, department number and salary of all employees who earn more than the average salary of their department

```
SELECT ename, deptno, salary
FROM employees E
WHERE salary >
    (SELECT AVG(salary)
    FROM employees
    WHERE E.deptno = deptno)
```

The letter *E* in the clause *where E.deptno = deptno* acts as a reference from the subquery to the outermost query. Thus *E.deptno* refers to *employees* in the outermost query. *Deptno* refers to *employees* in the subquery. This is effectively like manipulating two copies of the same table. One copy is used to calculate average salaries, the other is used as the basis of comparison for each employee.

3.3.7 Joins

SQL performs relational joins by indicating common attributes in the where clause of a *select* statement. For instance, the *select* statement below extracts data from the *employees* and *departments* tables of relevance to people working in department number 20.

Query:

'List the employee numbers, names, jobs and locations of all employees in department 20'

Statement:

SELECT empno, ename, job, location
FROM employees, departments
WHERE employees.deptno = departments.deptno
AND employees.deptno = '20';

Result:

Empno	Ename	Job	Location
7369	Smith	Clerk	Bristol
7566	Jones	Manager	Bristol
7788	Scott	Analyst	Bristol
7876	Adams	Clerk	Bristol
7902	Ford	Analyst	Bristol

3.3.8 Aliases

A column or table within the context of a query can be given another name known as an alias. Hence, for instance, we can give the table name *employees* the alias *E* in the following query and *departments* the alias *D*. This is achieved by appending the alias immediately after the table name.

SELECT empno, ename, job, location
FROM employees E, departments D
WHERE E.deptno = D.deptno
AND E.deptno = '20'

This technique is normally used to ease the keying-in involved in entering a query. It has however another more important purpose. Consider, for instance, writing a query to retrieve the names and salaries of all employees in the company who earn more than their managers. This can actually be done using the statement below.

SELECT ename, salary
FROM employees E, employees M
WHERE E.mgr = M.empno
AND E.salary > M.salary

In this statement two table aliases are assigned to the same table. This has the effect of setting up two copies of the same data for manipulation. In this case we have joined the *employees* table to itself by exploiting the fact that the *empno* column and the *mgr* column are defined on the same domain.

Another use for aliases involves assigning names to functions. Hence, in the following command we have given the average salary function a more presentable name.

> SELECT deptno, avg_salary avg(salary)
> FROM employees
> WHERE deptno IN (10,20)
> GROUP BY deptno

Result:

deptno	avg salary	COUNT(*)
10	2917	3
20	2175	5

3.3.9 Insert, Update and Delete

The type of data manipulation we have devoted primary attention to in this chapter has been passive in nature. In other words, we have assumed a database of facts which we have endeavoured to ask questions of.

There are however three other data manipulation commands in SQL which have a more active role. In other words, they are designed to enact changes to the state of the database itself. These commands are *insert*, *update* and *delete*.

3.3.9.1 The Insert Command

The simplest form of *insert* is used to add an extra row to a given table. For example,

> INSERT INTO departments
> VALUES ('50','Marketing','Cardiff')

The order in which values are listed in the *insert* statement should correspond to the order in which the columns were originally specified for the table in the *create table* statement.

If we do not wish to insert all the values of a particular row, or we wish to list the values in some order other than that originally specified, then we must add a list of column names to the *insert* statement. For instance,

```
INSERT INTO employees (job,ename,empno)
VALUES ('Clerk', 'Beynon', '2634')

INSERT INTO departments (deptno, dname)
VALUES('50', 'Marketing')
```

A variation of the *insert* command allows us to add multiple rows to a table. This is normally used as a means of loading up a given table with the results of some query. For instance,

```
CREATE TABLE salesmen
  (saleno NUMBER(4) NOT NULL,
   name CHAR(10),
   salary NUMBER(7,2),
   comm NUMBER(7,2),
   startdate DATE,
   dept NUMBER(2))

INSERT INTO  salesmen(number,name,salary,comm,start,dept)
   SELECT empno,ename,salary,comm,hiredate,deptno
   FROM employees
   WHERE job = 'Salesman'
```

3.3.9.2 The Update Command

The *update* command is used to modify the contents of one or more rows of a table. The relevant rows are specified by an optional *where* clause. The change or changes to be made to the rows are specified by a *set* clause. For example,

```
UPDATE employees
SET salary = salary * 1.1
```
Give everybody a 10% rise

UPDATE EMPLOYEES
SET salary = salary + 1000
WHERE deptno IN
  (SELECT deptno
    FROM departments
    WHERE dname = 'Research')
Give everybody in Research a £1,000 bonus

UPDATE departments
SET dname = 'R & D',Location = 'Edinburgh'
WHERE deptno = '20
Change the name of the research department and relocate it to Edinburgh

3.3.9.3 The Delete Command

The *delete* command is used to remove rows from a table. The actual rows to be deleted are specified by a *where* clause similar to that used in the *select* statement. The following examples delete one, three and all the rows of a table respectively. The last statement should obviously be used with extreme care !

DELETE FROM employees
WHERE ename = 'Clarke'

DELETE FROM employees
WHERE job = 'Salesman'

DELETE FROM employees
WHERE hiredate > '01-JAN-79'

3.3.10 Query Optimisation

The data retrieval facilities of SQL are close to what we might expect from a non-procedural query language. By this we mean that the user can express a retrieval request in SQL largely in terms of what he requires from the database. He does not need to get heavily involved in traversing or navigating through the database as he would using a hierarchical or network DBMS. To emphasise this point consider the two queries below. One is expressed in SQL, the other is expressed in a pseudo-DML close to those used in network products.

```
GET FIRST employees WHERE salary < 20000;
WHILE DB_status = 0 DO
    BEGIN
      WRITELN(employees.ename);
      GET NEXT employees WHERE salary <  20000;
    END;


SELECT ename
FROM employees
WHERE salary < 20000;
```

The SQL statement is made up of table names, column names and some matching condition. The network statement is made up of a series of read commands encased in a loop with an appropriate terminating condition. *DB_STATUS* is a system variable which is set to 1 when the end of file is reached. In this sense, the network version is a procedure - a set of statements expressed in some sequence. It is analogous to procedures expressed in such high-level languages as C.

Since computers are procedural machines, any statement expressed in non-procedural terms must eventually be translated into some procedural form. For any one non-procedural query, however, there are usually numerous different ways of achieving the same results procedurally. Hence, some mechanism must choose between the various procedural alternatives in terms of some notion of the best transformation for the job. Such a translation mechanism is known as a query optimiser (see figure 3.12).

To illustrate the function of a query optimiser let us consider an example. Suppose we want a list of all the names of people in the research department. We might express this in SQL using the following statement:

```
SELECT ename
FROM employees E, departments D
WHERE E.deptno = D.deptno
AND D.dname = 'Research'
```

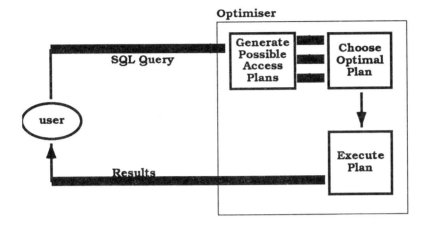

Figure 3.12

This statement may be translated into the relational algebra in a number of ways. Let us consider two. First, we may decide, for instance, to *join employees* to *departments* on *deptno*. Then we could perform an algebraic *select* to extract tuples for the research department. Finally, we would project out the list of employee names. In contrast, we might decide to do a *project* first of employee names and department numbers from the *employees* file. Then we could *equi-join* these two-column tuples to the *departments* file using a suitable restriction. Finally we might *project* out the employee names.

SQL is frequently described as being a database sub-language with in-built redundancy particularly in its data retrieval aspect (Date, 1989). By this it is meant that a given logical query such as - *find all the names of persons in the research department* - can be expressed in a number of different ways. Above we expressed this logical query as a relational join. Below we express the same logical query but this time exploiting the power of the subquery idea.

```
SELECT ename
FROM employees
WHERE deptno =
    (SELECT deptno
     FROM departments
     WHERE dname = 'Research')
```

The important point about this inherent redundancy in SQL is that one expression of a logical query is likely to be faster than another. In other words, it is possible to influence the performance of queries expressed in SQL by phrasing them appropriately. Depending upon your DBMS some things may be good to do, whereas others may have a prohibitive effect upon performance. As an illustration, we present a table of comparisons for the ORACLE DBMS.

These	**are faster than**	**These**
indexed columns		un-indexed columns
unique indexes		non-unique indexes
rowid = \<constant\>		any other search

Rowid is a system column maintained for every row in the database which is normally transparent to the user. It uniquely addresses a given row in a table and can therefore be used to access a row directly.

3.4 Conclusion

Data manipulation is the active part of any data model. Data manipulation concerns how data is entered into a database, how data is modified within a database, and how data is removed from a database. By far the largest aspect of data manipulation we have considered in this chapter is how data is retrieved from a database. We began by considering how the Relational Algebra acts as the theoretical basis for modern-day relational query languages. We then illustrated how the data manipulation language of SQL implements the operators of the Relational Algebra. We concluded with an examination of query optimisation, ie, the process of transforming statements expressed in some non-procedural language into a procedural interpretation.

3.5 Exercises

(1) Define data manipulation.

(2) What is the major defining characteristic of the operators of the Relational Algebra?

(3) Which operator of the Relational Algebra is said to be non-commutative?

(4) Write relational algebra statements to satisfy the following queries:

(a) Give me the employee record for Jones.

(b) Give me a list of department numbers.

(c) What is the name of employee number 7788?

(d) Give me the names of everybody in Research.

(5) What does the *structure* in Structured Query Language refer to?

(6) Why would we describe the Relational Algebra as being procedural whereas we would describe SQL as being non-procedural?

(7) Write SQL statements to satisfy the queries in question 4 above.

(8) Write a SQL query to list the average salary of members of the accounts department.

(9) Modify the personnel database in the following ways:

(a) Move all the managers to a table of their own

(b) Raise the commission levels of salesmen by 15%.

Chapter 4
Data Integrity

4.1 What is Data Integrity?

When we say a person has integrity we normally mean we can trust what that person says. We assume, for instance, a close correspondence between what that person says he did and what he actually did.

When we say a database has integrity we mean much the same thing. We have some trust in what the database tells us. There is a close correspondence between the facts stored in the database and the real world it models. Hence, in terms of our personnel database we believe that the fact - *Scott is a member of the Research department* - is an accurate reflection of the workings of our enterprise.

The issue of database or data integrity is probably the most explosive growth area in Relational Database Systems. Relational products have been traditionally poor at supporting integrity mechanisms. As we shall see, products have been poor even at supporting the inherent integrity rules of the Relational Data Model. Nevertheless, progress has been, and is being made. We shall discuss in this chapter, for instance, extensions to the SQL standard which are directly addressing these issues.

4.2 The Data Model

Let us review first an earlier distinction made between inherent and additional integrity. Inherent integrity is built into the data model itself. To be truly relational a database must satisfy the two inherent integrity rules of the Relational Data Model - *entity* and *referential integrity.*

Any information system cannot however rely on inherent integrity mechanisms alone. Some people have estimated that as much as 80 per cent of most commercial information systems are concerned with maintaining integrity (Martin, 1984). Any valid information system building tool must therefore have many more integrity mechanisms than are necessary to support inherent integrity. This is what we mean by additional integrity.

The concepts of inherent and additional integrity can therefore be closely linked with the two interpretations of the term data model discussed in chapter 2. Inherent integrity is located in the concept of data model as data architecture. Additional integrity is located within the concept of data model as a real world model - a set of enterprise rules. Inherent integrity is clearly limited in its ability to capture all the necessary connotations of integrity necessary within the latter definition of a data model (see figure 4.1).

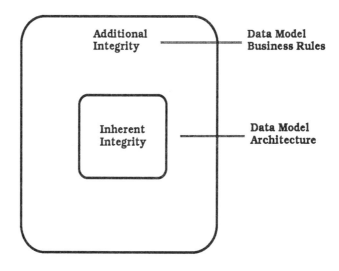

Figure 4.1

4.2.1 Entity Integrity

Entity integrity concerns primary keys. Entity integrity is an integrity rule which states that every table must have a primary key and that the column or columns chosen to be the primary key should be unique and not null.

Hence, in our employees table, *empno* is a valid choice as a primary key, *job* is not. Each value of *empno* is distinct, whereas there are a number of entries of the value *salesman*, for instance, in the *employees* table.

A direct consequence of the entity integrity rule is that duplicate rows are forbidden in a table. If each value of a primary key must be distinct no duplicate rows can logically appear in a table.

4.2.2 Referential Integrity

Referential integrity concerns foreign keys. The referential integrity rule states that any foreign key value can only be in one of two states. The usual state of affairs is that the foreign key value refers to a primary key value of some table in the database. Occasionally, and this will depend on the rules of the business, a foreign key value can be null. In this case we are explicitly saying that either there is no relationship between the objects represented in the database or that this relationship is unknown.

Take the case of our personnel database again. At first sight we observe only one foreign key - *deptno* in *employees*. By examining the *employees* table in detail we can verify that each employee has a *deptno* value, and that each *deptno* value corresponds to a value existing in the *departments* table. In this case we can say that the relationship between the object *employee* and the object *department* (in the direction of employee to department) is definite or deterministic. Every employee is assigned to a department. No employee record has a null *deptno* value.

Let us assume for the sake of argument however that the rules of this business change. The company decides to take on a large number of trainee employees. Each new recruit is obliged to undertake an induction tour of each company department before taking up his permanent departmental position. For such persons it is decided that that their *deptno* value will be null until they are assigned to a department.

Note above that we identified only one foreign key in the personnel database - at first glance. There is in fact one more- *mgr*. *Mgr* is unusual in that it is a foreign key to the primary key of the same table - *empno*. *Empno* and *mgr* are defined on the same domain - the set of all possible employee numbers. This type of relationship is said to be a recursive relationship.

4.2.3 When Can a Foreign Key be Null?

Let us assume we have two tables - *customers* and *orders* - representing the core of an order processing system.

Customers

Custno	Cname
1001	Goronwy Galvanising
1123	Peters Pies
1242	Corona Crisps
4002	Titan Tankers
..	..
..	..

Orders

Orderno	Custno	Orderdate
111	1001	01/01/90
112	1123	01/01/90
113	1123	02/01/90
114	4002	03/01/90
..	..	..
..	..	..

In this order-processing system we enforce the rule that an order cannot be taken for a non-existent customer. I.e., the customer details must be on the company's database before we can take orders from the company. In this case, the foreign key *custno* in the *orders* table cannot be null.

Let us consider another example, part of a stock control system which maintains details about *products* and *suppliers*.

Suppliers

Suppno	Sname
AZ101	Widgets inc.
AT112	The Woggle co.
BZ124	Wiggles
..	..
..	..

Products

Prodno	Desc	Suppno
2243	Widget	AZ101
2456	Woggle	AT112
2875	Wangle	
..	..	..
..	..	..

In this case, the relationship between *suppliers* and *products* is somewhat looser than that between *orders* and *customers*. Note that we have no supplier for product number 2875. Hence, it is a rule of our stock control system that a product on file may temporarily lack a main supplier. The foreign key *suppno* in *products* can therefore be null.

4.2.4 Maintaining Referential Integrity

Maintaining referential integrity in a relational database is not simply a case of defining when a foreign key should be null or not. It also entails defining what should happen when we add a record to a set of related tables, when we update a record, or when we delete a record.

Deletion is probably the most critical question so we concentrate on this issue here. Update and insertion follow on similar lines.

For every relationship between tables in our database we should define how we are to handle deletions of target and related tuples. In our personnel database, for instance, if we delete a row from the *departments* table (our target table) we must decide what should happen to related rows in the *employees* table. That is, what should happen to employees of the deleted department? Three possibilities are normally discussed:

(1) *Restricted Delete.* This is the cautious approach. It means we forbid the deletion of the department row until all employee rows within that department have been deleted.
(2) *Cascades Delete.* This is the confident approach. If we delete a department row all associated employee rows are deleted as a matter of course.
(3) *Nullifies Delete.* This is the middle approach. If we delete a department row we set the department numbers of relevant employees to null.

Let us assume that our organisation specifies a nullifies delete for the relationship between *employees* and *departments*. But what about some appropriate deletion specifications for the examples we considered in section 4.2.3?

In the case of *orders* and *products* we might specify a cascading delete. In other words, if we delete a customer record then all associated order records are deleted from the database. In the case of *suppliers* and *products* we might specify a restricted delete. That is, we do not delete a supplier record until all the products recorded against that supplier are erased.

4.2.5 Concurrency and Consistency

In section 4.2 we distinguished between two major types of integrity: inherent and additional integrity. These two types of integrity are concerned with the logical state of some database. The overall objective of both inherent and additional integrity is to make sure that some database is an accurate reflection of the real world it is attempting to represent. To these two major types of integrity we should add a third type which we shall choose to call base integrity. Base integrity is concerned with the physical dimension of a database system. In other words, base integrity concerns itself with the problems of hardware and software failure or the problems of distributing a scarce resource amongst multiple users. In this section we examine the two primary components of base integrity: ensuring concurrent access, and ensuring the consistency of some database.

An immediate consequence of the data sharing property of database systems is that mechanisms must be provided for handling concurrent access.

Consider the following problem. *User A* accesses *Allen's* employee record at time t1. *User B* however also accesses *Allen's* record at time t2. *User A* upgrades *Allen's* salary by 10% at time t3. *User B* upgrades his salary by 8% at time t4. The problem is that *user A's* update will have been lost since *user B's* update will have overwritten it. This is normally referred to as the lost update problem.

The conventional approach to handling the lost update problem is to maintain system locks. When a user locks a table or row of a table he is saying to other users, *I am doing something with this table or row, wait until I have completed my task.* The net result of applying locks is to serialise access to limited resources.

A related problem to that of concurrency is that of consistency. By consistency we mean the process of ensuring that a set of related actions are performed together or not at all. The classic case of the need for consistency arises in the banking arena. Here we have to ensure that a debit from one person's account is elsewhere recorded as a credit to someone else's account. We must not have the situation arising in which a debit is made but no credit arises.

Consistency is normally achieved by declaring logical units of work or transactions to the system. The system then ensures that a transaction either completes successfully or fails. A successful transaction is one in which all the operations of the transaction have completed successfully. A failed transaction is one in which one or more of the related operations within the transaction have not completed successfully.

4.3 The DBMS

Data integrity mechanisms, particularly in the areas of inherent integrity, fall some way short of fulfilling the integrity needs of the relational model in practice. We devote much of the remaining part of this chapter to examining some of these shortcomings, particularly with reference to ORACLE.

4.3.1 Entity Integrity in ORACLE

Entity integrity has to be enforced indirectly within ORACLE. In other words, we have to assign the *not null* characteristic to the primary key column and create a unique index on this column. This indirect method was discussed in chapter 2. The example below indicates how we would declare a primary key for the *departments* table.

```
CREATE TABLE departments
        (deptno NUMBER(2) NOT NULL,
         dname CHAR(10),
         loc CHAR(10))

CREATE UNIQUE INDEX dept_ind
ON departments(deptno)
```

4.3.2 Entity Integrity in DB2

Like ORACLE, most contemporary implementations of SQL do not have any direct means for specifying entity integrity. IBM's relational product, DB2, is an exception (Wiorkowski, 1988). In DB2 we can add a primary key specification to a create table statement. This looks likely to be adopted in the SQL2 standard (ISO, 1989). The example below illustrates how we might do this for the *employees* and *departments* tables.

```
CREATE TABLE employees
        (empno NUMBER(4),
        ename CHAR(10),
        job CHAR(9),
        mgr NUMBER(4),
        hiredate DATE,
        salary NUMBER(7,2),
        comm NUMBER(7,2),
        deptno NUMBER(2))
    PRIMARY KEY (empno)


CREATE TABLE departments
        (deptno NUMBER(2),
        dname CHAR(10),
        loc CHAR(10))
    PRIMARY KEY (deptno)
```

4.3.3 Referential Integrity in ORACLE

There is no current way of representing referential integrity directly within an ORACLE database. Referential integrity is left primarily up to the good practice of the Database Administrator (DBA). In other words, the DBA will record somewhere in the documentation of the database which columns comprise foreign keys and to which tables they refer. He will also normally establish a code of conduct as far as maintaining foreign key values are concerned and implement access constraints via data control mechanisms such as those to be discussed in chapter 5.

Hence, for instance, in terms of our personnel database we establish that *deptno* is a foreign key and that *mgr* is a recursive foreign key. We further establish that for our enterprise *deptno* cannot be null whereas *mgr* can. In other words, every employee must have a department, but there is at least one employee, the president, whio does not have a manager. We therefore place a *not null* declaration against the *deptno* column of *employees*. We also create two indexes on *mgr* and *deptno* in order to speed up the performance of *join* operations.

```
CREATE TABLE employees
    (empno NUMBER(4) NOT NULL,
    ename CHAR(10),
    job CHAR(9),
    mgr NUMBER(4),
    hiredate DATE,
    salary NUMBER(7,2),
    comm NUMBER(7,2),
    deptno NUMBER(2) NOT NULL)

CREATE TABLE departments
    (deptno NUMBER(2) NOT NULL,
    dname CHAR(10),
    loc CHAR(10))

CREATE INDEX deptf_ind
ON employees(deptno)

CREATE INDEX dept_ind
ON employees(mgr)
```

Note these are not unique indexes. We do not want to prohibit employees from having the same manager or department number.

4.3.4 Referential Integrity in DB2

Referential integrity is achieved in DB2 (and in SQL2) via foreign key specifications (Wiorkowski, 1988). The specifications below restrict the deletion of a department record until all matching employee records have been deleted. They also specify that any change made to the department number of a departments record should be reflected in all relevant employee records.

```
CREATE TABLE departments
        (deptno NUMBER(2),
        dname CHAR(10),
        loc CHAR(10))
```

PRIMARY KEY (deptno)

```
CREATE TABLE employees
        (empno NUMBER(4),
        ename CHAR(10),
        job CHAR(9),
        mgr NUMBER(4),
        hiredate DATE,
        salary NUMBER(7,2),
        comm NUMBER(7,2),
        deptno NUMBER(2))
    PRIMARY KEY (empno)
    FOREIGN KEY (deptno identifies departments,
        DELETE OF deptno RESTRICTED,
        UPDATE OF deptno CASCADES)
```

4.3.5 Consistency in ORACLE

In ORACLE, as in most SQL-based products, a transaction is simply a sequence of SQL statements that is packaged as a single entity. ORACLE maintains consistency by ensuring either that all the statements in a transaction complete successfully or that none do. In other words, if a transaction is made up of a deduction of money from one bank account and an addition to another bank account, then either both updates succeed or both fail.

In ORACLE the statements *commit* and *rollback* are used to delineate transactions. *Commit* makes permenant changes to a database. *Rollback* undoes all changes made in an unsuccessful transaction. Hence, if our transaction is made up of the two updates discussed above, and for some reason a system failure occurred after the first update, issuing a *rollback* command will take the database back to its previous state. Conversely, if we are happy that our banking transaction has completed successfully, issuing a *commit* command will make the updates permanent.

Some commands such as *create table* and *create index* automatically commit when they are executed. For most other commands the default is not to commit. This system-wide edict can be changed however by the command *set autocommit on*. This has the effect of commiting all changes immediately after the execution of an SQL statement.

4.3.6 Concurrency in ORACLE

ORACLE maintains three types of locks: share, share update and exclusive locks:

A *share lock* allows other users query access to a table but prohibits update access. In other words, you apply this type of lock when you wish to query a table but you do not want to change it. Also, you do not wish other users to change it while you are looking at it. Any other user can apply a share lock to the same table.

A *share update lock* allows users to have both query and update access to a defined set of rows of a table.

An *exclusive lock* is similar to a share lock except in one important respect. Only one user can declare an exclusive lock on a table at any one time.

4.4 The Developing Integrity Issue

Data integrity is probably the most developing area of relational database systems. Current relational products can be expected to offer direct support for inherent integrity in the relatively near future. Support for additional integrity is likely to take a while longer. Some RDBMS, such as INGRES, already offer some support for additional integrity, but there is still a long way to go (Stonebraker, 1986). In this section we take a brief look at the future for integrity mechanisms in RDBMS.

4.4.1 Active Data Dictionaries

A data dictionary is a repository for meta-data. The classic data dictionary is a passive repository. In other words, the first data dictionaries were built as systems external to a database. They were systems built to record the complexities of a given database structure for use by application development staff and DBAs.

If we equate the term data dictionary with the set of system tables as discussed in chapter 2, then a data dictionary in a relational system is an active repository. It is an inherent, internal part of the database system designed to buffer the user from the base tables.

Many people believe however that the system tables available in most SQL-based products are inherently limited in functionality (Codd, 1990). In particular, They wish to see the inclusion of some representation of inherent and additional integrity mechanisms within the data dictionary.

Traditionally, integrity issues have been external to the database system. Integrity has primarily been the province of application systems written in languages such as COBOL or C which interact with the database. Programs are written in such languages to validate data entered into the database and ensure that any suitable propagation of results occurs.

Many have argued however that the logical place for integrity is within the domain of the data dictionary under control of the DBMS. The argument is that integrity cannot be divorced from the underlying database. Two or more application systems interacting with one database may enforce integrity differently or inconsistently. Hence, there should be only one central resort for monitoring integrity. Integrity should be the responsibility of the DBA. Mechanisms should be available therefore for the DBA to define and enforce integrity via the DBMS.

We have already discussed how the present generation of relational products are addressing the inherent integrity rules of the relational data model. Much work still needs to be done however to produce truly effective mechanisms in this area. Once the inherent integrity issue has been suitably handled, the next logical step is to include mechanisms for enforcing additional integrity constraints via the DBMS.

When the stage at which additional integrity is incorporated within the realms of the DBMS this engine changes somewhat in nature. No longer is it correct to call it a tool for managing a database or a set of databases. The DBMS becomes more of a tool for application building. It is not suprising therefore to find the world of fourth generation languages melding with the realm of relational systems. Figure 4.2 summarises the developing role of the data dictionary concept.

4.4.2 Support for Additional Integrity

What sort of mechanisms will be needed for additional integrity? We look at three main types in this section - assertions, triggers and alerters

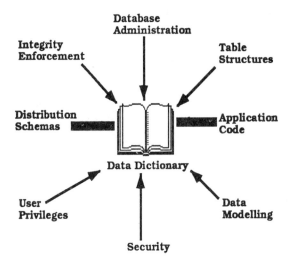

Figure 4.2

(Beynon-Davies, 1990).

An *assertion* is simply a rule expressed on a database. Suppose we wished to ensure, for example, that all managers earned more than £1800 per month. We might express this as an assertion in a pseudo-SQL syntax as follows.

```
CREATE ASSERTION a1
ON employees
DEFINE FORALL employees
    (IF employees.job = 'Manager'
    THEN
    employees.salary > 1800)
```

This assertion would be checked every time a change is made to the employees file. If a new manager record is attempted to be inserted into the table, for instance, that record will be thrown out unless the condition of the assertion is satisfied.

Assertions are passive integrity mechanisms. They are created merely to prohibit certain states of a database from occuring. *Triggers* are active integrity mechanisms. They are used to propagate a string of associated updates throughout the database. Suppose, for instance, we maintain somewhere in our database a tally of the total number of employees for quick reference. The following trigger will update this tally every time a new employee record is inserted.

```
CREATE TRIGGER t1
ON INSERT OF employees
UPDATE tally
SET total_emp = total_emp + 1
```

An *alerter* is a variant of the trigger mechanism. Rather than causing changes of the database to occur, an alerter notifies specific users of happenings in the database. The following alerter notifies a user named *beynon* of an employee earning more than £3000 per month.

```
CREATE ALERTER r1
ON UPDATE OF employees
    INSERT OF employees
WHERE salary > 3000
ALERT beynon
```

4.4.3 A Standard Information Resource Dictionary System

We discussed in chapter 2 how a data dictionary forms an integral part of any relational database system. We have also discussed in this chapter how in recent years the data dictionary concept, particularly the idea of a data dictionary system, has been continually expanded. Data dictionary systems now contain information about programs, users, hardware and corporate information strategy (Navathe, 1986). Such systems are no longer data dictionary systems in the true sense of the word. They are more accurately referred to as Information Resource Dictionary Systems (IRDS). An IRDS might be defined as a centralised repository of information about all the information resources relevant to some organisation. Figure 4.3 illustrates the role of the IRDS.

In 1984, the American National Standards Institution (ANSI) produced a draft standard for the IRDS concept. This achieved full standard status in 1989 (ANSI, 1989c). The standard specifies a core system of facilities found in most contemporary data dictionary systems.

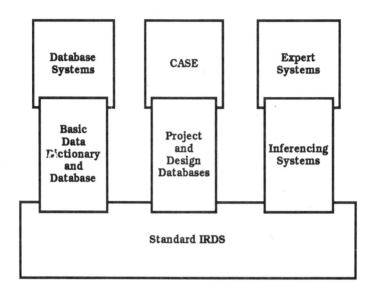

Figure 4.3

Around this core ANSI specifies a series of optional modules such as an application program interface and security module (Dolk, 1987 and Goldfine, 1985).

The architecture of the standard IRDS is based on an alternative data model to the relational data model known as the Entity-Relationship model (Chen, 1976). In this model, which we shall discuss in chapter 8, the user sees the dictionary as being made up of *entities*, *relationships* and *attributes*. An entity is merely a named thing of interest such as a *file*, *program* or *user*. A relationship is a named association between entities. Hence, *system-contains-program* and *user-responsible-for-system* are two valid relationships between entities in the standard IRDS. Attributes are properties of entities or relationships. Hence, *date-created*, *description* and *comments* are all valid attributes of a *program* entity. *Access-method*, likewise, is a valid attribute of the relationship *program-processes-file*.

The standard IRDS is intended to define the ways in which an organisation controls and monitors its information resource. One output from the IRDS, for instance is an impact-of-change report. This report will list all entities affected by a change to one or more entities in the system.

Hence, for instance, the system can be used to document a change of referential integrity constraints between files in a database.

4.5 Conclusion

Data integrity is the process of ensuring that a database remains an accurate reflection of the real world it is attempting to model. Data integrity comes in three forms: base, inherent and additional. Base integrity is about recovery mechanisms from hardware and software failure. Inherent and additional integrity fall into the area of data modelling. Inherent integrity is related to the concept of data model as architecture. Additional integrity is related to the concept of data model as a set of business rules. Although we have concentrated on the two inherent integrity rules of the relational data model, we have also discussed how data management systems are developing into the area of additional integrity.

Data integrity is probably the most important way of ensuring that a database remains an accurate reflection of the real world situation it is attempting to represent. The other important mechanisms contributing to this goal are grouped together under the heading of data control. It is to this topic that we now turn in chapter 5.

4.6 Exercises

(1)   Define data integrity.
(2)   Why do you think data integrity is one of the most explosive growth areas in relational database products?
(3)   Distinguish between inherent and additional integrity.
(4)   Define entity integrity.
(5)   Define referential integrity.
(6)   How do we decide the question of when a foreign key can be null?
(7)   Distinguish between a restricted delete, cascading delete and nulli fies delete.
(8)   Which of these three types of delete do you think is handled the most easily by a DBMS, and why?
(9)   How is entity integrity enforced in SQL?
(10)   Why do you think that CASE and the question of data integrity are inextricably linked?

(11)   What is an alerter, trigger and assertion?

(12)   What do you think are the benefits of a standard for dictionary
            systems?

Chapter 5
Data Control

5.1 What is Data Control?

In any multi-user system, some person or persons have to be given responsibility for allocating resources to the community of users and monitoring the usage of such resources. In database systems, two resources are of pre-eminent importance: data and DBMS functions. Data control is the activity which concerns itself with allocating access to data and allocating access to facilities for manipulating data. Data control is normally the responsibility of the database administrator (DBA).

In this chapter we shall examine some of the fundamental aspects of data control in relational database systems. First, we shall examine the concept of a relational view. Second, we shall discuss how DBAs manipulate the view concept in order to allocate access to data. Third, we shall examine the DBAs ability to allocate access to DBMS functions such as data definition.

5.2 The Data Model

Until relatively recently, data control had not been an explicit part of the relational data model. The concept of a database view however has become of such importance to database practice that a great deal of literature now exists on the subject.

5.2.1 Views

A view is a virtual table. It has no concrete reality. No data is actually stored in a view. A view is simply a window into the database. It presents to the user a particular perspective on the real world represented by the database. Figure 5.1 illustrates how a view named *research* is formed from data held in the *employees* and *departments* tables.

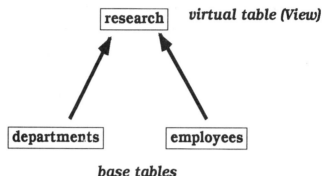

base tables

Figure 5.1

Figure 5.2 illustrates two further views on the *employees* table. *EmpA* is a view which gives *UserA* access to employee numbers, names, salaries and hire dates. *EmpB* is a view given to *UserB* allowing him to access details of department numbers, and jobs of employees.

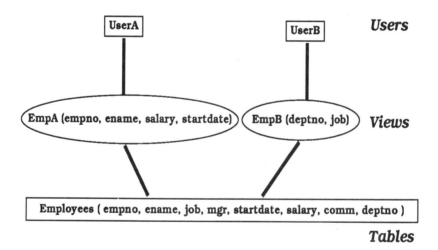

Figure 5.2

5.2.2 Three Uses for Views

We can identify three main uses for views in a database system: to simplify, to perform some regular function, or to provide security.

The two views described in the previous section illustrate the simplification purpose. Suppose these two views are designed for use by personnel clerks. *EmpA* is designed for use by clerks monitoring company pay policy. *EmpB* is used by clerks monitoring departmental rolls. These views allow us to simplify the underlying database structure and display only the data the clerks need to perform their function.

There is an implicit edict in the relational model: *store as little as possible*. One consequence of this is that any data that can be derived from other data in the database is not normally stored. If, for instance, there is a requirement to regularly display the ages of employees we would not store both a person's age and their birthdate. A person's age can be derived from a person's birthdate. The view mechanism is the conventional means for performing such computations and displaying them to the user.

We shall consider the question of security in some detail in section 5.3.6. Suffice it to say here that if we make the analogy between a view and

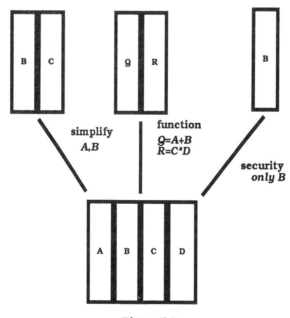

Figure 5.3

a window, we can make windows as big or as small or as complicated as we want. Hence, the view mechanism is a major tool in the hands of the database administrator for controlling database access.

Figure 5.3 illustrates these three uses for views.

5.2.3 Updating through Views

Retrieving information through views is a straightforward process. It involves merging the original query on the view with the view definition itself. File maintenance operations such as insertion, deletion, and update are however more complex to accomplish via views, and hence deserve more consideration.

The main point is that not all views are updatable. Consider, for instance, *EmpA* and *EmpB*.

In the case of *EmpA*, for instance, we can perform the following operations:

(1) Insert a new row into the view. For example *1234, Beynon, 10-JAN-82*. What would normally happen is that a record padded out with nulls would be written to the underlying *employees* table.

(2) Delete an existing record from a view. For instance, *7499, Allen, 17-DEC-80*. The corresponding row in the base table would be deleted.

(3) Update an existing field in the view. For example change Allen's hiredate.

In the case of *EmpB* problems arise:

(i)   Suppose we wished to insert a record for a new clerk, eg, *10, clerk*. We would have to insert the record *null, null, clerk, null, null, null, 10* into the underlying *employees* table. This attempt will fail since employee number (the table's primary key) must not be null.

(ii) Suppose we wish to update a record, eg, *10,clerk* to *20,clerk*. How do we identify the relevant record to update?

(iii) The same applies to deletion. Any attempt to delete a record via the view *EmpB* is likely to be ambiguous.

On closer examination, the main difference between *EmpA* and *EmpB* lies in the fact that *EmpA* contains the primary key column and *EmpB* does not. This means that updates to *EmpA* unambiguously update rows in a view. Updates to *EmpB* are frequently ambiguous.

5.2.4 Commands for DBAs

In any database system, the database administrator needs to be able to do three main things:

(1)   Prevent would-be users from logging on to the database
(2)   Allocate access to specific parts of the database to specific users
(3)   Allocate access to specific operations to specific users.

In section 5.3 we shall examine SQL's capability for handling the second of these needs. In considering the first and third need we shall resort to examining the facilities available under the ORACLE RDBMS.

5.3   The DBMS

The view concept has been an established part of SQL since its early days at IBM. We also cover in the sections that follow the *grant* and *revoke* commands available to users of DBA status.

5.3.1 The CREATE VIEW statement

A view in SQL is a packaged *select*. The syntax is as follows:

        CREATE VIEW <view name>
        AS <select statement>

The following two examples create the *EmpA* and *EmpB* views discussed in section 5.2.1:

        CREATE VIEW empa AS
        SELECT empno, ename,salary
        FROM employees

        CREATE VIEW empb AS
        SELECT ename,deptno,job

FROM employees

When a view has been created, it can be queried in the same manner as a base table. For instance:

SELECT *
FROM empa
WHERE salary < 1600

Result:

EMPA

Empno	Ename	Salary
7369	Smith	800
7521	Ward	1250
7654	Martin	1250
7844	Turner	1500
7876	Adams	1100
7900	James	950
7934	Miller	1300

5.3.2 Examples

(1)   A view of special interest to *Blake*, the sales manager:

CREATE VIEW sales AS
    SELECT empno, ename, salary, comm
    FROM employees
    WHERE job = 'Salesman'

(2)   A view implementing a *join*:

CREATE VIEW london AS
    SELECT empno, dname
    FROM employees E, departments D
    WHERE E.deptno = D.deptno
      AND loc = 'London'

(3)   A view exploiting aggregate functions.

        CREATE VIEW stats AS
            SELECT deptno, MIN(salary), AVG(salary), MAX(salary)
            FROM employees
            GROUP BY deptno

5.3.3 Updating through Views in SQL

In section 5.2.3 we discussed how certain views are not updateable and how certain other views are updateable. In this context, C. Date has made the distinction between three types of views (Date, 1989):

(1)   Views which are updateable in theory and in practice
(2)   Views which are updateable in theory, but not yet in practice
(3)   Views which do not appear to be updateable in theory and therefore cannot be updateable in practice.

Figure 5.4 summarises these three types of view.

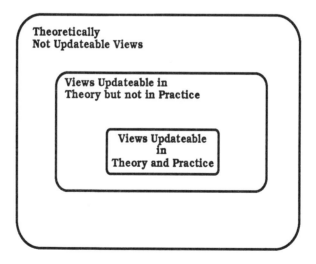

Figure 5.4

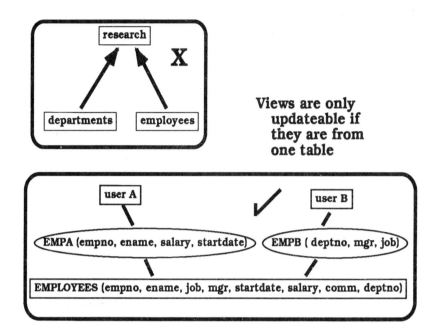

Figure 5.5

Since this section concerns the practical implementation of relational constructs we need only consider views which are updateable both in theory and in practice. What then defines the first type of view? As far as most SQL-based systems are concerned the following conditions have to be satisfied (ORACLE, 1987a):

(1)   The *select* clause in a view cannot use a *distinct* qualifier or any function definition.
(2)   The *from* clause must specify just one table. No joins are allowed.
(3)   The *where* clause cannot contain a correlated subquery.
(4)   The *group by* and *order by* clauses are not allowed.
(5)   No *union* operator is permitted.

According to these criteria the view *research* in figure 5.5 is invalid. Since both *empa* and *empb* are extracts from a single underlying table both these views are valid.

5.3.4 GRANT and REVOKE

SQL provides two commands for controlling access to data. One command gives access privileges to users. The other command takes such privileges away.

To give a user access to a view or a table we use the *grant* command.

GRANT [ALL : SELECT : INSERT : UPDATE : DELETE]
ON [<table name> : <view name>]
TO <user name>

For example,

GRANT INSERT ON employees TO pbd
GRANT SELECT ON empa TO pbd

To take existing privileges away from a user we use the *revoke* command.

REVOKE [ALL : SELECT : INSERT : UPDATE : DELETE]
ON [<table name> : <view name>]
FROM <user name>

For instance,

REVOKE INSERT ON employees FROM pbd
REVOKE SELECT ON empa FROM pbd

5.3.5 Granting Access via Views

One of the best ways of enforcing control in relational database systems is via the view concept. Let us suppose, for instance, that we wish to give *Jones* the ability to look at and update the records of employees in the department he manages - *Research*. We do not however wish to give *Jones* the ability to delete employee records or insert new employee records. This is to be the responsibility of the central personnel department. To enact these company rules we create a view:

```
CREATE VIEW research AS
    SELECT *
    FROM employees
    WHERE deptno =
    (SELECT deptno
    FROM employees
    WHERE ename = 'Jones')
```

This view looks as follows:

Research

Empno	Ename	Job	Mgr	Hiredate	Salary	Comm	Deptno
7369	Smith	Clerk	7902	17-DEC-80	800		20
7566	Jones	Manager	7839	02-APR-81	2975		20
7788	Scott	Analyst	7566	09-NOV-81	3000		20
7876	Adams	Clerk	7788	23-SEP-81	1100		20
7902	Ford	Analyst	7566	02-DEC-81	3000		20

Note that the employee record for *Jones* is included in this view. If we now provide *select* and *update* access for *Jones* as below:

```
GRANT SELECT, UPDATE
ON research
TO jones
```

this particular manager will be able to change his own salary ! There are a number of ways we can prevent this happening by modifying the view definition. One possible solution is given below:

```
CREATE VIEW research AS
    SELECT *
    FROM employees
    WHERE deptno =
        (SELECT deptno
        FROM employees
        WHERE ename = 'Jones')
    AND ename <> Jones
```

5.3.6 DBA Privileges in ORACLE

In sections 5.3.1 to 5.3.5 we have considered how SQL permits the DBA to specify access to parts of the database and how it permits the DBA to associate these allocations with particular users. However, at present SQL does not contain a definition of how users are declared to the database system in the first place, and also how such users are given access to various DBMS facilities. Assigning users and giving such users access privileges are two DBA functions which vary from product to product. To give the reader a flavour for the type of mechanisms available, we discuss here the facilities available under ORACLE (ORACLE, 1987b).

5.3.7 Users, User Names and Passwords

We define a user as some person authorised to access the database via the DBMS. In most DBMS, a user is known to the database system by his or her user name. This is a string of characters which the person must type in response to a logon prompt.

Associated with a given user name we usually find a password. This is another string of characters which must be typed by the person wishing to gain access. Unlike a user name however a password being entered is not usually echoed back to the user's screen. The other major difference between user names and passwords is that passwords are normally under the control of a given user. They can be changed by the user at any time. User names however are normally created by the DBA and can only be modified by him alone.

5.3.8 CONNECT, RESOURCE and DBA

When a company receives a new ORACLE system it comes automatically installed with two users: *sys* and *system*. The *sys* user owns all the system tables. The *system* user owns all the views of the data dictionary. The first thing the DBA does is change the default passwords for these user names. The second thing he does is start enrolling users into the system.

To declare an ORACLE user the DBA must normally supply three pieces of information: a distinct user name, a password, and the level of privilege granted to the user.

There are three classes of ORACLE user: *connect, resource* and *dba*.

Connect is the lowest level of privilege. It allows the user to access the oracle DBMS, look at other users' data if allowed, perform data manipulation tasks specified by the DBA, and create views. *Resource* privilege allows the user to create database tables and indexes and grant other users access to these tables and indexes. *Dba* privilege is normally given to a chosen few. The *sys* and *system* users discussed above have *dba* privileges. Such privileges permit access to any user's data, and allows the granting and revoking of access privileges to any user in the database.

When a new user is enrolled into the system the database administrator grants the user one or more of these privileges using the command below:

        GRANT {CONNECT : RESOURCE : DBA}
        TO <username>
        [IDENTIFIED BY <password>]

For example,

        GRANT CONNECT, RESOURCE
        TO pbd
        IDENTIFIED BY croeso

In a similar manner to granting database access as discussed in section 5.3.4, DBMS privileges can be revoked as below:

        REVOKE {CONNECT : RESOURCE : DBA}
        FROM <username>

For instance,

        REVOKE CONNECT, RESOURCE
        FROM pbd

5.4 Conclusion

We began this chapter by defining data control as the activity devoted to controlling access to data and DBMS functions. Data control is normally the responsibility of the database administrator.

In Relational Database Systems, the data aspect of data control revolves around the concept of a view. A view is a virtual table. Views can be used to create windows in a database which can be allocated to specific users of the database.

The DBMS-side of data control varies from product to product. Most RDBMS however have facilities for assigning user names and passwords to users and defining the overall privileges available to users.

5.5 Exercises

(1) Define the term data control.
(2) What makes a view different from a base table?
(3) What are the three main purposes of the view concept?
(4) Why are some views not updateable?
(5) What types of views are updateable in SQL?
(6) Create a view of all employees in the same department as Allen.
(7) Create a view of all employees sited in London.
(8) Assuming that we have added an age column to the employees table, create a view of all employees within five years to retirement age 65.
(9) Let King have every type of access to the records of his managers.
(10) Let Miller have *select* access on all London-based employees.

Chapter 6
Data Analysis

6.1 What is Data Analysis?

In chapter one we discussed two meanings of the term data model. This is a term used to refer either to an architecture for data or to a model of the workings of some enterprise or part of some enterprise. Data analysis concerns itself with the latter interpretation. Data analysis is the process of building a business data model and representing it as a relational schema. Data analysis is also referred to as logical database design.

6.2 Approaches to Data Analysis

There are normally held to be three complementary approaches to doing data analysis: top-down, bottom-up and laterally (more conventionally known as view integration).

Doing data analysis top-down means we use a diagramming technique such as Entity-Relationship diagramming to map what we believe to be the

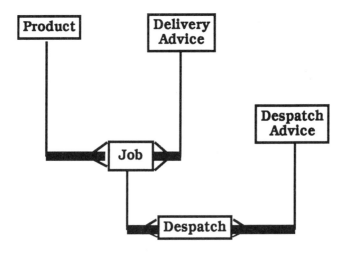

Figure 6.1

things of interest to the enterprise and the relationships between these things of interest. Top-down data analysis is frequently referred to as conceptual modelling because we remain at a high-level or on a fairly abstract plane. The product of such a modelling exercise is usually an Entity-Relationship diagram such as the one shown in figure 6.1. This diagram can be transformed into a set of table-structures - a relational schema - via a straightforward process of translation or accommodation. Entity-Relationship diagrams are also used in lateral data analysis. Here a series of differing viewpoints collected from various members of the organisation are plotted. These viewpoints are then integrated by super-imposing each upon the other and attempting to reach a state of compromise. The eventual model can be translated into a relational schema via a similar process as for top-down data analysis.

Rather than dealing with abstract concepts, bottom-up data analysis deals with concrete data. To do bottom-up data analysis we must have a pool of data items, extracted probably from an examination of existing enterprise documentation. To this pool of data items we apply a series of transformation rules. Bottom-up data analysis is also called normalisation.

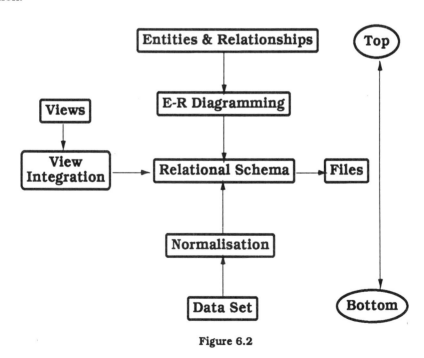

Figure 6.2

Figure 6.2 summarises these three different approaches to data analysis.

6.3 The Advantages of Normalisation

Suppose we are given the brief of designing a database to maintain information about patients and wards in a General Hospital. An analysis of the documentation presently used by the hospital gives us the following sample data set with which to work. If we pool all the data together in one table as below, a number of problems would arise in maintaining this data set.

Ward Name	Ward Type	No of Beds	Sister	Patient No.	Patient Name	Date of Birth
Bryn Siriol	Paediatric	6	N Hughes	3424	J Beynon	05-JAN-87
Bryn Siriol	Paediatric	6	N Hughes	2567	T Jones	10-MAR-88
Bryn Siriol	Paediatric	6	N Hughes	6789	R Burton	21-APR-89
Cefn Coed	Geriatric	8	T Evans	4545	F Davies	05-MAR-05
Cefn Coed	Geriatric	8	T Evans	3434	E Evans	10-OCT-10
Merthyr	General	10	M Thomas	2344	R Collier	10-JUN-67

(1)   What if we wish to discharge patient *R Collier?* The result is that we lose some valuable information. We lose information about *Merthyr* ward. This is called a deletion side-effect.

(2)   What if we transfer patient number *6789* into intensive care? We need to update not only the ward type but also the name of the ward, its sister and the number of beds. This is called an update side-effect.

(3)   What if we admit a new patient, say *7777, G Vaughn* to the *Orthopaedics* ward? We need to know more information, namely about the *Orthopaedics* ward. This is an insertion side-effect.

(4)   We change the position of the sister *N Hughes.* She transfers from *Paediatrics* to the *General* ward. We now have to update 3 different records in the file. This is an update side-effect again.

The size of our sample file is small. One can imagine the seriousness of the file-maintenance anomalies mentioned above multiplying as the size of the file grows. The above organisation is therefore clearly not a good organisation for the data of this enterprise. Normalisation is a formal process the aim of which is to reduce file maintenance anomalies.

6.4 Approaches to Normalisation

There are at least two approaches to normalisation. The traditional method, first espoused by Codd (Codd, 1970), and enhanced by numerous other researchers (Dutka,1989), uses a step-by-step approach to database design. This approach has proven an excellent vehicle for explicating the intricacies of Relational Database design. It suffers as a practical design method however in that it is extremely difficult to apply a series of step-by-step transformations to a large data set.

In this chapter we shall therefore concentrate on an alternative technique which exploits the advantages arising from the use of diagrams. The technique, known variously as determinancy diagramming or dependency diagramming is a practical, two-step process for producing a good database design. In the first step, we build up, in an iterative manner, a diagram representing the relationships between data-items. In the second step, we take the completed diagram and apply a series of well-defined rules to arrive at a relational schema.

6.5 Determinancy Diagramming

Because the data structures of relational database systems are simple, a relational database will suffer from numerous file maintenance problems unless it has been subject to a number of good design principles. These design principles are conventionally bundled together as a series of five steps known as normal forms. Beginning with an unnormalised database the first guideline is applied to give us a database in first normal form. Then the second guideline is applied to give us a database in second normal form, and so on. The entire process of transforming an unnormalised database into a fully normalised database is frequently referred to as a process of non-loss decomposition, since we continually fragment our database structure into more and more tables without losing the fundamental relationships between data-items (Beynon-Davies, 1989).

Although non-loss decomposition does yield a database design free from file maintenance problems, it does require an initial data-set to be in place before the process can begin. Also, for any reasonably large data-set the process is extremely time-consuming, difficult to apply, and prone to error.

The following sections describe a contrasting approach to database design which uses a graphical notation to transform an evolving set of unstructured data-items simply and directly into fully normalised tables. Being graphical in nature it is easier to use and less prone to error than the step-by-step procedure described above.

6.5.1 Determinancy and Dependency

Normalisation is the process of identifying the logical associations between data-items and designing a database which will represent such associations but without suffering the file maintenance anomalies discussed in section 6.3. The logical associations between data-items that point the database designer in the direction of a good database design are referred to as determinant or dependent relationships. Two data-items, A and B, are said to be in a determinant or dependent relationship if certain values of data-item B always appear with certain values of data-item A.

Determinancy also implies some direction in the association. If data-item A is the determinant data-item and B the dependent data-item then the direction of the association is from A to B and not vice versa.

6.5.2 Functional and Non-Functional Dependency

There are two major types of determinancy or its opposite dependency: functional, sometimes referred to as single-valued determinancy, and non-functional, or multi-valued determinancy. In the text which follows we give some formal definitions for these two types of determinancy with associated examples.

Functional Determinancy. Data-item B is said to be functionally dependent on data-item A if for every value of A there is one, unambiguous value for B. In such a relationship data-item A is referred to as the determinant data-item, while data-item B is referred to as the dependent data-item.

Non-Functional Determinancy. Data-item B is said to be non-functionally dependent on data-item A if for every value of data-item A there is a delimited set of values for data-item B.

Example 1. In our personnel database, *empno* and *ename* are in a functional determinant relationship. *Empno* is the determinant and *ename* is the dependent data-item. This is because for every employee number there is only one associated value of employee name. For example, *7369* is associated with the value *Smith*. This does not mean to say that we cannot have more than one employee named *Smith* in our organisation. It simply means that each *Smith* will have a different employee number. Hence, although there is a functional determinancy from employee number to employee name the same is not true in the opposite direction - employee name does not determine employee number.

Example 2. Staying with the *employees* table, employee number functionally determines department number. For every employee there is only one associated department number which applies.

Example 3. In the *departments* table *deptno* functionally determines *loc*. Every department is sited at just one location.

Example 4. Consider now adding an extra data-item to our personnel database - *employee skill*. Let us assume that our company maintains a large, coded list of human skills relevant to the company. The company wishes to record which employees have which skills. Clearly the relationship between employee numbers and skills is not a functional determinancy. Some employees may just have one skill, but most will have two or more skills.

Empno and *skill* are in a non-functional or multi-valued determinancy. In other words, for every *empno* we can identify a delimited set of skill codes which apply to that employee.

Example 5. The same is true for the data-item *dependent name*. Many employees will have just one dependent but most will have two or more. *Empno* and dependent name is in a multi-valued or non-functional dependency.

Example 6. Finally, let us consider the case in which we wish to record, particularly for those working in the research department, the projects these employees are working on. The important point that this example emphasises is that determinant relationships are fundamentally business rules. One company may enforce the rule that an employee is assigned to only one project at any one time. Hence, in this company, the relationship between employee number and project number is a functional one. In another organisation the rule may be that an employee can be assigned to more than one project, but perhaps no more than three projects at one time. This makes the relationship between employee number and project number a multi-valued determinancy.

6.5.3 Notation

A diagram which documents the determinancy or dependency between data-items we shall refer to as a determinancy or dependency diagram. Data-items are drawn on a determinancy diagram as labelled boxes. Functional dependency is represented between two data-items by drawing a single-headed arrow from the determinant data-item to the dependent data-item. For example, figure 6.3 represents a number of functional relationships as determinancy diagrams.

Many valued or non-functional dependency is indicated by drawing a double-headed arrow from the determinant to the dependent data-item. Figure 6.4 represents two non-functional relationships as determinancy diagrams.

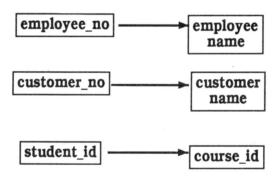

data-item B is functionally dependent on data-item A if for every value A there is only one distinct and associated value for B

Figure 6.3

data-item B is non-functionally dependent on data-item A if for any single value of A there is an associated set of values for data-item B

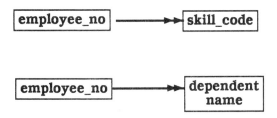

Figure 6.4

6.5.4 *Transitive Dependency*

Consider the following simple table.

Manager	Department	Location
Evans	Accounts	Cardiff
Jones	Marketing	Newport
Davies	Research	Swansea
Thomas	Production	Bridgend

By examination, we can identify three functional determinancies in this table, one from *manager* to *department*, one from *department* to *location*, and one from *manager* to *location*. On consideration however what we have in this table is a transitive determinancy. In other words, any situation in which A determines B, B determines C and A also determines C can be simplified into the chain A to B and B to C. Identifying transitive determinancies can frequently simplify complex determinancy diagrams. Figure 6.5 illustrates this process.

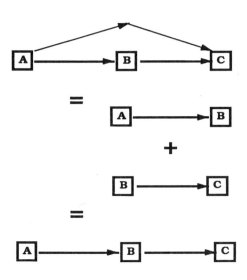

Figure 6.5

6.5.5 Accommodation

In this section we examine the process of transforming a determinancy diagram into a set of table structures or relational schema, a process frequently known as accommodation.

Suppose we are given the determinancy diagram in figure 6.6. We transform the diagram in figure 6.6 into a set of table structures by applying two rules, one rule for each type of determinancy.

(1)   Every functional determinant becomes the primary key of a table. All immediate dependent data-items become non-key attributes of the table. This is frequently referred to as the Boyce-Codd rule after its inventors.

(2)   Every non-functional determinant becomes part of the primary key of a table. That is, we make up a compound key from the determinant and dependent data-items in a non-functional association.

To represent the relational schema we use a notation sometimes known as the bracketing notation. We list a suitable mnemonic name for the table first. This is followed by a list of data-items or column names delimited by commas. It is conventional to list the primary key for the table first and

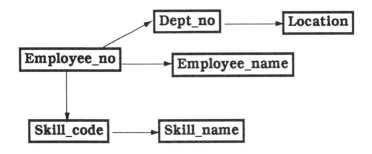

Figure 6.6

underline this data item. If the primary key is made up of two or more attributes, we underline all the component data items.

<relation name> (<u>primary key</u>, <column name>, ...)

Applying the functional and non-functional dependency rules to the diagram in figure 6.6 gives us the following table structures in the bracketing notation.

Employees(<u>employee-no</u>, employee_name, dept_no)
Departments(<u>dept-no</u>, location)
Employee_Skills(<u>employee-no, skill code</u>)
Skills(<u>skill code</u>, skill_name)

6.6 Advantages of Determinancy Diagramming

The main advantage of the determinancy diagramming technique is that it provides a mechanism for designing a database incrementally. One does not need a complete data-set in hand to begin the process of design. The data analyst can begin his work with a small collection of central data-items. Around this core data-items can be continuously added until the dependencies are fully documented.

6.7 Example: Criminal Court Cases

In this section we shall illustrate the principles discussed in the previous sections by way of one example. A further example is given in the case study in appendix 4.

Let us suppose that we are given the brief of designing an information system for the scheduling of criminal court cases. We begin by attempting an initial analysis of the data presently held in manual form. We pool the information gleaned from an examination of documentary sources in one unnormalised table as below.

Judge No.	Judge Name	Case No.	Start Date	Court	Def. No.	Def. Name	Crime	Def. Counsel	Pros. Counsel
01	Farqhuar	569	01/09/89	C1	2456	I.Vaughn	Car Theft	Davies	Smythe
02	Jennings	325	01/09/89	C2	2457	T.Smith	Burglary	Evans	Raleigh
02	Jennings	325	01/09/89	C2	2459	C.Burgh	Burglary	Beynon	Raleigh
01	Farqhuar	576	21/02/90	C2	3001	R.Davy	Rape	Beynon	Smythe
03	Gordon	603	21/09/89	S1	3012	G.Basle	GBH	Evans	Raleigh
03	Gordon	603	21/09/89	S1	3013	T.Evans	GBH	Evans	Raleigh
03	Gordon	666	01/11/89	S2	3056	R.Thomas	Fraud	Evans	Raleigh
03	Gordon	890	01/01/90	S2	3111	I.Blythe	Exposure	Davies	Smythe
02	Jennings	9000	01/01/90	C1	4021	T.Johns	Fraud	Beynon	Smythe

Our aim now is to document the determinant relationships between data items in this table. We find, for instance, that there is a functional dependency between *judge number* and *judge name*. Every time *03* appears in our table the judge name *Gordon* appears also. In fact, all the relationships between data items in our table can be mapped in functional terms. A determinancy diagram produced from the table above is given in figure 6.7.

The next step is to translate this diagram into a relational schema. Since all the relationships are functional, we can use the Boyce-Codd rule throughout to give us 3 table structures as below.

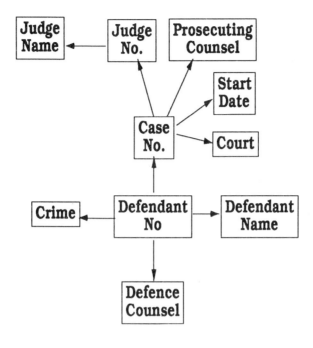

Figure 6.7

Judges(<u>judge-no</u>, judge_name)
Cases(<u>case-no</u>, start_date, court, pros_counsel, judge_no)
Defendants(<u>def-no</u>, def_name, crime, def_counsel)

6.8 Conclusion

We began this chapter by defining data analysis as the process of producing a logical database design. We then considered the three complementary approaches to data analysis: Entity-Relationship diagramming, Normalisation and View Integration. Bottom-up data analysis or Normalisation was chosen to illustrate the process of database design via a technique known as determinancy diagramming. The technique was demonstrated on a small case study. A larger case study discussed in appendix four places this technique within the context of implementing a Relational Database System.

6.9   Exercises

(1)   Define the term data analysis.

(2)   Why is normalisation described as a bottom-up approach to data analysis.

(3)   What are the primary advantages of a normalised database?

(4)   Why is a diagramming approach to normalisation preferable to a step-by-step approach?

(5)   Distinguish between functional determinancy and non-functional determinancy.

(6)   What is accommodation?

(7)   Draw a determinancy diagram from the table below. Convert the determinancy diagram into a set of table structures.

Course ID	Course Name	Lecturer ID	Lecturer Name	Student ID	Student Name	Grade
23	Databases	12	D.Shephard	101	S.Bashar	A
24	Expert Systems	13	D.Mcphee	101	S.Bashar	A
35	Logic	11	G.Rees	102	G.Rees	B
35	Logic	11	G.Rees	101	S.Bashar	C
45	Compilers	12	D.Eyres	102	G.Rees	C
45	Compilers	12	D.Eyres	103	T.Takhar	A

(8)   Construct a set of table structures from the determinancy diagram below.

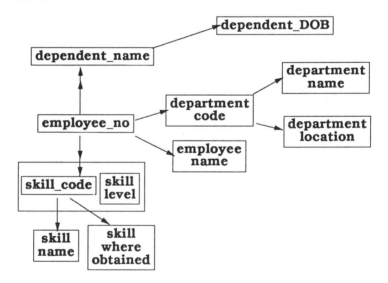

Figure 6.8

Chapter 7
Application Development

7.1 Introduction

In this chapter we add further flesh to our discussion of a representative Relational DBMS. The DBMS discussed in previous chapters was primarily based around the documentation of the 1987 SQL standard and its implementation in ORACLE. In this chapter we highlight further aspects of ORACLE to illustrate the developing nature of database products in the relational world. The specific theme is the way in which relational DBMS products are no longer simply tools for database management. They are application development environments.

7.2 The ORACLE Kernel and Toolkit

Modern day relational DBMS generally come in two parts, which we shall refer to as the kernel and the toolkit. The kernel comprises the core DBMS functions generally implemented in some dialect of SQL. Around this

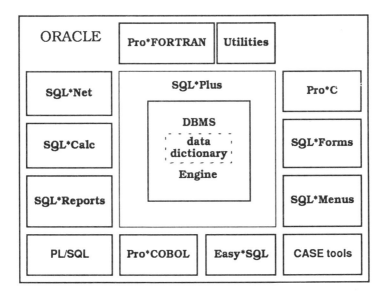

Figure 7.1

standard interface most vendors offer a range of additional software tools for producing information systems. Thus the concept of DBMS originally discussed in chapter one is extending ever further outwards to encompass more and more areas of application building.

Figure 7.1 illustrates the architecture available from the ORACLE corporation. The kernel comprises a relational database engine and a standard interface known as SQL*Plus (ORACLE, 1987a). Around this kernel a range of products are offered. These comprise a forms-based application development tool, SQL*Forms (ORACLE, 1987c), a tool for producing system menus, SQL*Menus, a spreadsheet facility, SQL*Calc, a tool for networking systems, SQL*Net, a report-writer, SQL*Report, and a number of links to third generation languages the most developed of which is to C, PRO*C. Version 6 of ORACLE also encompasses a procedural 4GL known as PL/SQL and a set of CASE tools based around entity-relationship diagramming.

In this chapter we discuss three parts from this development environment: first, the ability to embed SQL statements in a language such as C; second, the ability of SQL*Plus to act as a report-writer; finally, how SQL*Forms can be used to build interfaces for information systems. The whole objective of this chapter is to give the reader a feel for the potential for application development via relational database systems.

7.3 Embedded SQL

SQL comes in two forms. It can either be used interpretively or it can be embedded within a host language such as COBOL, FORTRAN, PL/1, C, or PASCAL. It is the former usage that we have devoted most attention in this work. The latter usage is primarily for application developers. It is designed to simplify database input and output from application programs via a standard interface. In this section we introduce the concept of SQL as an embedded database language by discussing one simple example in a pseudo-host language modelled on PASCAL.

```
PROGRAM emp_names;
VARIABLES empno: integer;
BEGIN
      EXEC SQL DECLARE employees CURSOR FOR
            SELECT  empno
```

```
        FROM employees;
    PRINT 'Employee Numbers';
    PRINT '_____';
    EXEC SQL OPEN employees;
    EXEC SQL FETCH employees INTO :empno;
    WHILE SQLCODE = 0 DO
        PRINT empno;
        EXEC SQL FETCH employees INTO :empno;
    EXEC SQL CLOSE employees
END
```

The program above prints the list of employee numbers in the *employees* table. Embedded data language statements are preceded by the keywords *exec sql.* The *declare* statement defines a pointer to the *employees* table known as a cursor. When the *open* statement is activated, the *select* statement defined at the declare stage is executed. This creates a copy of all the employee numbers in the base table and places it in a workspace area. To retrieve an actual record from this workspace we use the *fetch* command. The *fetch* statement takes an employee number and places it in a program variable *empno*, indicated by the colon. *Sqlcode* is a system variable. It returns 0 if the *fetch* executed successfully, non-zero otherwise. Hence we use it here to act as a terminating condition to traverse the employee numbers in the workspace.

The concept of a *cursor* is extremely important in that it acts as the cement between the inherently non-procedural nature of SQL and the inherently procedural nature of a third generation language such as Pascal. There is in fact what is usually referred to as an impedance mismatch between SQL and 3GLs. SQL, being relational, works at the file level. It takes tables as input and produces tables as output. 3GLs however work at the record level. They only process one record at a time. We therefore have to have some mechanism of translating from a file-based to a record-based approach. This is provided by the cursor.

A program written in this hybrid manner is normally submitted to a pre-compiler. The *exec sql* keywords are important in enabling the pre-compiler to identify SQL commands from Pascal commands. The pre-compiler will take the SQL commands and create a database access module. It will also take the Pascal commands and produce a source program suitably modified with database access calls. This modified

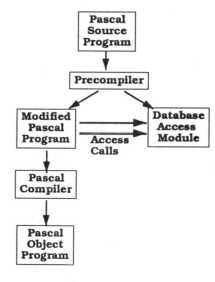

Figure 7.2

source is then compiled in the normal manner. Figure 7.2 illustrates this:

7.4 Interpreted SQL

The normal way of experiencing SQL is in interpreted mode. In this section
we look at how SQL*Plus works in interpreted mode. The first thing the
user has to do is logon to SQL*Plus. This he can do using the following
command:

    $ SQLPLUS <username>/<password>

For example,

    $ SQLPLUS scott/tiger

Scott and *tiger* are a username and password available on all ORACLE
systems. They can be set up to contain a personnel database similar
to the one we have discussed throughout this work. We know we are
in SQL*Plus when we get the following prompt:
    SQL>

We can now type in a command line such as the following:

```
SQL> SELECT *
   2 FROM departments
```

Deptno	Dname	Location
10	Accounting	London
20	Research	Bristol
30	Sales	London
40	Operations	Birmingham

4 records selected

Note how we can spread a statement over several lines for ease of reading and for ease of editing. This is because SQL*Plus maintains a small working memory known as the SQL buffer. Anything we type in response to the SQL prompt gets stored in the buffer. The statement is not activated until we type a semi-colon to terminate the statement or issue the command *run*. Take for instance, the following sample dialogue which is meant to illustrate the use of the buffer for editing:

```
SQL>   LIST
    1 SELECT *
    2 FROM departments
SQL>   INPUT
    3 WHERE deptno = '10'
    4
SQL> LIST
    1 SELECT *
    2 FROM departments
    3 WHERE deptno = '10'
SQL> LIST 1
    1 SELECT *
SQL>   CHANGE/*/deptno,loc/
SQL>   LIST
    1 SELECT deptno,loc
    2 FROM departments
    3 WHERE deptno = '10'
SQL>   LIST 3
```

```
      3 WHERE deptno = '10'
SQL>   APPEND AND deptno = '20'
SQL>   LIST
      1 SELECT deptno,loc
      2 FROM departments
      3 WHERE deptno = '10' AND deptno = '20'
SQL> RUN
```

Deptno   Location

10   London
20   Bristol

2 records selected

7.5 SQL*Plus

SQL*Plus is ORACLE's dialect of the 1987 SQL standard. It contains all of the facilities specified in level 1 of the standard, most of level 2, and a few extensions not specified in the standard. In this section we shall

'A report is simply the result of a query, formatted to make it look more 'finished'

SELECT dname,ename, salary
FROM employees,departments
WHERE employees.deptno =
departments.deptno
AND deptno IN (10,20);

DNAME	ENAME	SALARY
Research	Smith	800
Research	Jones	2970
Accounting	Clark	2450
Research	Scott	3000
Accounting	King	5000
Research	Adams	1100
Research	Ford	3000
Accounting	Miller	1300

Figure 7.3

examine how SQL*Plus can be used as a report writer.

7.5.1 What is a Report?

In SQL*Plus a report is simply a query fringed with formatting commands to make the result look like a more finished product. Figure 7.3 illustrates a simple query in SQL. It must be remembered that the report formatting commands we shall discuss are commands within SQL*Plus - ORACLE's superset of the level 1 SQL standard (ANSI, 1986).

7.5.2 A Sample Report

Figure 7.4 illustrates the formatted result from the query expressed in figure 7.3. In the sections which follow we shall explore how to:

(1)   Change standard column headings
(2)   Change standard formats for columns
(3)   Add titles
(4)   Break ordered data up into suitable components for processing by aggregate functions

ACME ACCOUNTING & RESEARCH DEPARTMENTS

DEPARTMENT NAME	EMPLOYEE NAME	MONTHLY SALARY
Accounting	Clark	£2,572.50
	King	£5,500.00
	Miller	£1,300.00
*********************		---------------
sum		£9,372.50
Research	Smith	£920.00
	Jones	£3,123.75
	Scott	£3,795.00
	Adams	£1,265.00
	Ford	£3,450.00
*********************		---------------
sum		£12,553.75

Page 1

Figure 7.4

7.5.3 Column Headings

When a query's result is displayed, the column headings are taken from the table definitions stored in the system catalog. Such names are usually short and cryptic because of the length limitation imposed on column names by the DBMS. Fortunately, SQL*Plus allows us to extend the standard headings into something more meaningful via the column command. Figure 7.5 illustrates the use of this command on our sample query. Note that to display a heading over more than one line we use a

```
COLUMN dname HEADING 'DEPARTMENT:NAME';
COLUMN ename HEADING 'EMPLOYEE ' ;
SELECT dname,ename, salary
FROM employeess,departments
WHERE employees.deptno = departments.deptno
ANDdeptno IN (10,20);
```

DEPARTMENT NAME	EMPLOYEE	SALARY
Research	Smith	800
Research	Jones	2975
Accounting	Clark	2450
Research	Scott	3000
Accounting	King	5000
Research	Adams	1100
Research	Ford	3000
Accounting	Miller	1300

Figure 7.5

7.5.4 Print Formats

The column command can also be used to specify the display format for data in a table. Note how in the example in figure 7.6 we have specified a detailed numeric format for the salary column. Each 9 in the format

COLUMN dname HEADING 'DEPARTMENT:NAME';

COLUMN ename HEADING 'EMPLOYEE:NAME' ;

COLUMN salary HEADING 'MONTHLY:SALARY' FORMAT £9,999.99;

SELECT dname,ename, salary

FROM employees,departments

WHERE employees.deptno = departments.deptno

AND deptno IN (10,20);

DEPARTMENT NAME	EMPLOYEE NAME	MONTHLY SALARY
Research	Smith	£800.00
Research	Jones	£2,975.00
Accounting	Clark	£2,450.00
Research	Scott	£3,000.00
Accounting	King	£5,000.00
Research	Adams	£1,100.00
Research	Ford	£3,000.00
Accounting	Miller	£1,300.00

Figure 7.6

stands for an integer.

7.5.5 Titles

SQL*Plus has a series of commands of relevance to pagination. The most

COLUMN dname HEADING 'DEPARTMENT:NAME';

COLUMN ename HEADING 'EMPLOYEE:NAME' ;

COLUMN salary HEADING 'MONTHLY:SALARY' FORMAT £9,999.99;

TTITLE CENTER 'ACME WIDGET ACCOUNTS & RESEARCH DEPARTMENTS';

BTITLE RIGHT 'PAGE ' SQL.PNO;

SELECT dname,ename, salary

FROM employees,departments

WHERE employees.deptno

= departments.deptno

AND deptno IN (10,20);

ACME WIDGET ACCOUNTS & RESEARCH DEPARTMENTS		
DEPARTMENT NAME	EMPLOYEE NAME	MONTHLY SALARY
Research	Smith	£800.00
Research	Jones	£2,975.00
Accounting	Clark	£2,450.00
Research	Scott	£3,000.00
Accounting	King	£5,000.00
Research	Adams	£1,100.00
Research	Ford	£3,000.00
Accounting	Miller	£1,300.00
		PAGE 1

Figure 7.7

commonly used are *ttitle* and *btitle* - top title and bottom title respectively. In figure 7.7 we have specified a centred string as a heading. We have also specified a standard function as a bottom title, namely *sql.pno*. This automatically produces page numbers at the position specified.

7.5.6 Breaks

The *break on* command is used to organise the rows of a report into groups such that an appropriate action can be taken at the point intervening between such groups. Breaks are only relevant for use with ordered data. This means that we must have a SQL query containing either an *order by* or *group by* clause. In figure 7.8 we have chosen to order the data by department name. The *break on* command here is causing a blank line to appear. This is what the statement *skip 1* represents

COLUMN dname HEADING
  'DEPARTMENT:NAME';

COLUMN ename HEADING
  'EMPLOYEE :NAME' ;

COLUMN salary HEADING
  'MONTHLY:SALARY' FORMAT
  £9,999.99;

TITLE CENTER 'ACME
  WIDGET ACCOUNTING AND
  RESEARCH DEPARTMENTS';

BTITLE RIGHT 'PAGE '
  SQL.PNO;

BREAK ON dname SKIP 1;

SELECT dname,ename,salary

FROM employees, departments

WHERE employees.deptno

= departments.deptno

AND deptno IN (10,20)

ORDER BYdname;

ACME ACCOUNTING & RESEARCH DEPARTMENTS		
DEPARTMENT NAME	EMPLOYEE NAME	MONTHLY SALARY
Accounting	Clark	£2,572.50
	King	£5,500.00
	Miller	£1,300.00
Research	Smith	£920.00
	Jones	£3,123.75
	Scott	£3,795.00
	Adams	£1,265.00
	Ford	£3,450.00
		Page 1

Figure 7.8

7.5.7 Subtotals

Breaks are normally used as a means of performing needed computations. In figure 7.9, for instance, we have chosen to compute subtotals of salary relevant to each department. We could equally well have computed *min, max, avg, count* etc.

COLUMN deptno HEADING
  'DEPARTMENT:NAME';

COLUMN ename HEADING 'EMPLOYEE
  :NAME' ;

COLUMN salary HEADING
  'MONTHLY:SALARY' FORMAT
  £9,999.99;

TTITLE CENTER 'ACME
  WIDGET:ACCOUNTING & RESEARCH
  DEPARTMENT';

BTITLE RIGHT 'PAGE ' SQL.PNO;

COMPUTE SUM OF salary ON dname;

BREAK ON dname SKIP 1;

SELECT dname,ename,salary

FROM employees, departments

WHERE employees.deptno =
  departments.deptno

AND deptno IN (10,20)

ORDER BY dname;;

ACME ACCOUNTING & RESEARCH DEPARTMENTS		
DEPARTMENT NAME	EMPLOYEE NAME	MONTHLY SALARY
Accounting	Clark	£2,572.50
	King	£5,500.00
	Miller	£1,300.00
		-------------
sum		£9,372.50
Research	Smith	£920.00
	Jones	£3,123.75
	Scott	£3,795.00
	Adams	£1,265.00
	Ford	£3,450.00
		•-------------
sum		£12,553.75
		Page 1

Figure 7.9

7.5.8 Saving Reports

Reports are normally designed as standard queries to be run repeatedly
on the corporate database. In other words, they demand to be stored for

```
SQL> LIST
 1  COLUMN dname HEADING
    'DEPARTMENT:NAME";
 2  COLUMN ename HEADING 'EMPLOYEE:NAME ' ;
 3  COLUMN salary HEADING 'MONTHLY:SALARY'
    FORMAT £9,999.99;
 4  COMPUTE SUM OF salary ON dname;
 5  TTITLE  CENTER 'ACME WIDGET ACCOUNTING
    AND RESEARCH DEPARTMENTS';
 6  BTITLE  RIGHT 'PAGE ' SQL.PNO;
 7  BREAK ON dname SKIP 1;
 8  SELECT dname,ename,salary
 9  FROM employees, departments
10 WHERE employees.deptno =
    departments.deptno
11 AND deptno IN (10,20)
12 ORDER BY dname;
SQL> SAVE personnel;
SQL> CLEAR BUFFER;
```

Figure 7.10

use by various users of the database system. We can save the contents of the SQL buffer in an external file by using the *save* command with an appropriate filename. Figure 7.10 illustrates the process of saving our report.

7.6 SQL*forms

SQL*Forms is ORACLE's fourth generation application builder. Using SQL*Forms the developer can produce screens for data entry, data modification and query on any ORACLE database (ORACLE, 1987c).

7.6.1 Forms

A form is simply a data entry and retrieval interface to parts of a relational database. Figure 7.11 illustrates a simple form which we shall create for entry of departmental information.

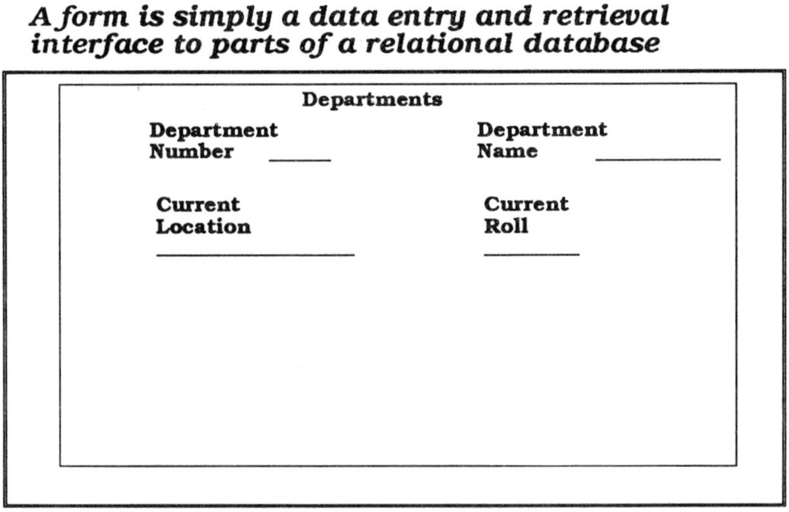

A form is simply a data entry and retrieval interface to parts of a relational database

Figure 7.11

7.6.2 Default Forms

The easiest way to create a form is to exploit information contained in the system tables. This is known as a default form. Here we describe how to create a default form from the information stored about the *departments* table.

```
┌─────────────────────────────────────────────────────────────┐
│ ┌───────────────────────────────┐                           │
│ │        CHOOSE FORM            │                           │
│ │ Name dept_entry               │                           │
│ │                               │                           │
│ │ Actions:                      │                           │
│ │  CREATE MODIFY   LIST         │                           │
│ │  RUN    DEFINE   LOAD         │                           │
│ │  FILE   GENERATE              │                           │
│ └───────────────────────────────┘                           │
│                                                             │
│                                                             │
│                                                             │
│                                                             │
│                                                             │
│                                                             │
│ Form:          Block:        Page:    SELECT:   Char Mode: Replace │
└─────────────────────────────────────────────────────────────┘
```

Figure 7.12

On entry to SQL*Forms the screen illustrated in figure 7.12 is displayed. The *choose forms* window is displayed in the top left-hand corner of the screen and the screen cursor is positioned after the *name* prompt. Each form in an application system must be given a unique name. We choose to call ours *dept_entry*.

Once a name has been entered one of the various actions indicated in

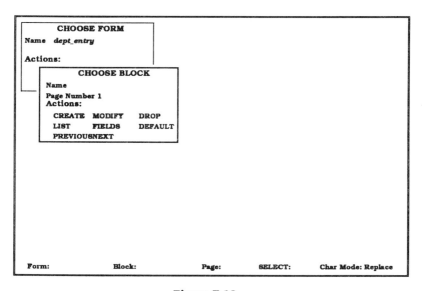

Figure 7.13

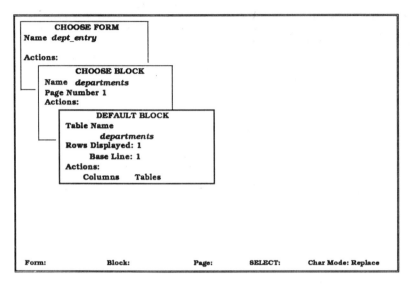

Figure 7.14

the window can be chosen or selected using keys pre-defined to SQL*Forms for your particular system. We first create the form by selecting this particular action. The *choose block* window then appears as in figure 7.13.

A block is a unit of a form corresponding to one underlying table from the database. Since we wish to build a form for entry of departmental information we enter the name of the *departments* table here. We then

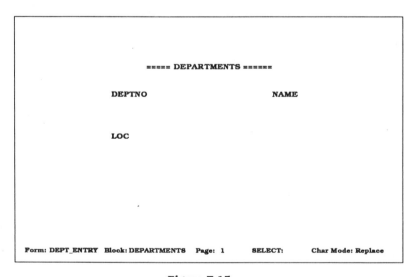

Figure 7.15

```
┌─────────────────────────────────────────────────────────┐
│ ┌─────────────────────────────────────────────────────┐ │
│ │                    Departments                      │ │
│ │      Department              Department             │ │
│ │      Number    ____          Name      _____     │ │
│ │                                                     │ │
│ │      Current                 Current                │ │
│ │      Location                Roll                   │ │
│ │      _____          _____               │ │
│ │                                                     │ │
│ │                                                     │ │
│ │                                                     │ │
│ │                                                     │ │
│ │                                                     │ │
│ └─────────────────────────────────────────────────────┘ │
└─────────────────────────────────────────────────────────┘
```

Figure 7.16

select the default action from the actions displayed in this window. The *default block* window appears as in figure 7.14.

Pressing the *accept* key causes the actions to be saved and the default block window to disappear. We are now back at the *choose block* window as in figure 7.13. This time we select the *modify* action. This causes a sample data entry screen to be displayed as in figure 7.15.

We are now in a screen painter. In other words, from this point we can change the way in which the data entry screen looks to the eventual user. We will simply change the names of the data items on the screen from the names appearing in the table structures to something more meaningful. Pressing the *accept* key means that the form displayed in figure 7.16 is saved.

7.6.3 Triggers

The form in figure 7.16 can now be generated and run. In practice however, many further additions will be made to a form such as this to make it a practicable data entry tool. The developer would usually add a series of triggers to the data entry form. SQL*Forms has a different idea of a trigger to that described in chapter 4. An SQL*Forms trigger encapsulates the definitions given there for assertions, triggers and alerters. In other words, a SQL*Forms trigger can be used to:

(1)   Enforce a passive integrity constraint such as department numbers shall be in the range 10 - 100.
(2)   Alert certain users of changes made to the *departments* file.
(3)   Cause the *employees* file to be updated appropriately whenever, for example, a department number is changed.

Figure 7.17 illustrates the way in which a trigger can be used to perform a function. Here we have added an extra field to our data entry form and associated with this field a *select* statement which extracts from the *employees* file the current roll of a particular department.

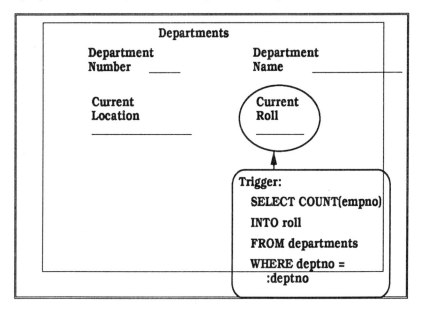

Figure 7.17

7.7 Conclusion: Building an Application

This chapter has illustrated the way in which relational database systems have now become an accepted tool for the development of information systems. The average data processing application is made up of the following elements:

(1) Data entry screens
(2) Data modification screens
(3) Reports
(4) Menus

Items (1) and (2) can be directly produced via SQL*Forms. Item (3) can be produced via SQL*Plus. Item (4) can be produced either in SQL*Forms or via an associated package known as SQL*Menus.

The alternative is to build an application using a conventional programming language such as C and embed database access into the program code using SQL.

7.8 Exercises

(1) Describe the difference between the kernel and toolkit ideas.
(2) Distinguish between interpreted and embedded SQL.
(3) For which group of users do you think embedded SQL is designed ?
(4) What's the impedance mismatch?
(5) What is a report in SQL terms?
(6) Describe the main functional components of an average application system.
(7) What advantage do you think SQL*Forms offers over development using embedded SQL?

Chapter 8
The Future of Relational Database Systems

8.1 Introduction

In this chapter we assess the future for database systems founded on the relational approach to database management. In the years since its invention, the relational data model in particular has been buffeted by a number of different trends in computing. We assess here only a few of perhaps the most important happenings that are likely to influence the future of Relational Database Systems.

We begin with an assessment of contemporary SQL, then move on to discuss three strands of computing that are heavily influencing the development of relational DBMS - semantic data models, object-oriented database systems and multi-media databases. This leads us to a discussion of the way in which particularly object-oriented ideas can be incorporated within relational systems. Finally, we conclude with a discussion of the way in which database systems are changing in nature. The database systems of today will be the knowledgebase systems of the future. Those interested in a more detailed discussion of these issues are referred to Beynon-Davies (1990).

8.2 A Historical Critique of SQL

SQL is undoubtedly becoming the standard interface to relational database systems. In many respects, it is attempting to define the standard functionality of a relational DBMS. Despite its increasing prominence however, SQL has probably had as many critics as it has had supporters. In this section we seek to summarise this debate by discussing some perceived problems of the database sub-language, as defined in the ANSI (1986)/ISO (1987) standard, and how these stimulated the developments, presently ongoing, for the development of SQL2.

8.2.1 The Advantages of SQL

Critics of SQL frequently lose sight of some noted strengths of the database sub-language. For instance,

(1)   SQL supports a major proportion of the Relational Data Model as originally expounded by Codd.

(2)   It combines all the standard file maintenance functions - table creation, update, amendment and deletion - with extras such as view definition, in one uniform syntax.

(3)   SQL can be used either as a standalone query language or embedded within a conventional programming language such as C.

(4)   SQL supports all the major relational retrieval operators - *select*, *project* and *join* - in a usable, non-procedural, form.

(5)   SQL supports to a certain extent the idea of program-data independence. Indexes may be added to tables, for instance, and removed from tables without impacting upon users or application programs.

8.2.2 The Disadvantages of SQL

After publication of the ANSI (1986)/ISO (1987) standard a number of papers by, most notably, E.F. Codd and C. Date heavily criticised the language (Codd, 1988a, 1988b and Date, 1987). The attempt was to formulate a critique not only of the standard but the limitations of database products at the time. The most cogent of these criticisms are given below. It is noteworthy that since ORACLE is most rightly seen as an implementation of the ANSI (1986) standard many of the criticisms still apply to this particular database product.

(1)   The ANSI (1986) SQL standard lacks a direct means for declaring primary keys. It therefore lacks any direct mechanism for supporting entity integrity. This is related to Codd's major criticism of SQL - that it permits, by default, duplicate rows in a table.

(2)   The ANSI SQL (1986) standard also lacks a means for declaring foreign keys. It thereby has no inherent mechanism for enforcing referential integrity.

(3)   The ANSI SQL (1986) standard does not have a user-friendly mechanism for storing the temporary results of queries. The nested sub-query idea which was originally designed for this purpose has been heavily criticised for being too cumbersome.

(4)   Some relational algebraic operations such as *division* are not supported. Others, such as *union*, are implemented in what many regard as an unnatural fashion.

(5)   Null values are treated in what many see to be an arbitrary way by
       the in-built functions of SQL. For instance, nulls are eliminated in
       the computations of such functions as *sum* and *avg*. In the function
       count(*) however nulls are included.

8.2.3 The Debate

The list above is by no means complete. C. Date, for instance, has heavily
criticised SQL for its built-in redundancy or lack of orthogonality (Date,
1989). By this he means that, in many instances, there is more than one
way of writing an SQL query. Others have praised this feature of the
language pointing to the creative nature by which humans exploit
redundancy (Beech, 1989). The list in section 8.2.2 should therefore be
treated merely as a selection from the major elements of the debate.

The debate itself continues and acts as a major catalyst for affecting
changes in the SQL standard. Since 1986 a number of revisions have been
made to the standard that Codd and Date originally addressed their
criticims. Hence, for instance, it is expected that the new ISO standard for
SQL2 will include a *primary key* and *foreign* key function similar to those
discussed in chapter four for DB2. The standard will also contain other
elements like a *create domain* statement, also discussed in chapter four.
These extensions go some way to addressing the major point at issue: the
ability of SQL to implement relational constructs (see figure 8.1).

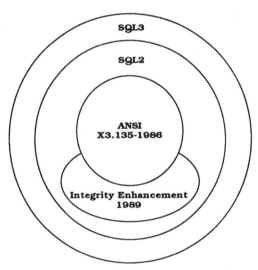

Figure 8.1

8.2.4 Why a Standard for SQL?

SQL is becoming the standard interface to relational databases and is progressively moving towards fulfilling many of the properties of the relational data model as proposed by theoreticians like Codd and Date. The major point at issue is: do we need a standard for relational database management anyway?

A number of advantages are certainly likely to arise from a standard in this area. For instance:

(1)   Reduced costs for retraining application developers in the intricacies of database products

(2)   Applications developed via a database system can run unchanged (relatively) on a number of different hardware and software platforms

(3)   Applications developed using a standard language are likely to have a longer lifespan than those developed using a non-standard language

(4)   Standards facilitate communication between not only database systems but also information systems built on database languages.

However, there is one big problem with any standard. Standards by their very nature stifle creativity. A *standard* relational database language does not mean the *best* relational database language. One cogent point made by C. Date, for instance, is that SQL has never been formally designed (Date, 1989). In other words, it has never been subject to the principles of formal language design. Codd believes that this characteristic of SQL has an important consequence for the future of relational database systems. He believes that only a language based on formal, logical, principles is likely to provide a firm enough basis for the database demands of the year 2000 and beyond (Codd, 1990).

8.3 Semantic Data Models

Data models are undoubtedly central to information systems work in two senses. First, they provide the conceptual basis for thinking about applications of a data-intensive nature. Second, they provide a formal basis for the tools and techniques of information systems building.

Brodie has made a distinction between three generations of data model (Brodie, 1984):

(1) *Primitive Data Models*. In this approach objects are represented by record-structures grouped in file structures. The main operations available are read and write operations over records. Third generation languages such as COBOL, at least in terms of a minimal definition of COBOL, primarily use primitive data models.

(2) *Classic Data Models*. These are the hierarchical, network and relational data models. The hierarchical data model is an extension of the primitive data model discussed above. The network is an extension of the hierarchical approach as defined by CODASYL. The relational data model is a fundamental departure from the hierarchical and network approaches.

(3) *Semantic Data Models*. The main problem with the classic data models is that they still maintain a fundamental record-orientation (King and Mcleod, 1985). In other words, the meaning of the information in the database - its semantics - is not readily apparent from the database itself. Semantic information must be consciously applied by the user of databases using the classic approach. Semantic data models attempt to provide a more expressive means of representing the meaning of information than is available in the classic models.

In this section, we aim to give the reader a basic understanding of what the term semantic data model means and what semantic data models have to offer over and above the relational data model (King and Mcleod, 1985).

8.3.1 The Problem of Semantics

The relational data model has undoubtedly proved an effective conceptual modelling tool for database work. A great deal has been published however, even by Codd himself, about the deficiencies of modelling the real world in relational terms (Codd, 1979). Many argue that the relational data model does not offer a sufficiently rich set of constructs for this activity. This accounts for the publication of a large number of alternative data models over the last two decades (Peckham, 1988). This set of alternative data models is loosely categorised as the set of semantic data models since their single unifying characteristic is that they aim to provide more meaningful content (semantics) than the relational data model.

Consider, for instance, the table below:

10	Bryn Siriol	6	N. Hughes
12	Cefn Coed	8	T. Evans
15	Merthyr	10	M. Thomas
20	Rhondda	12	G. Jones

The only thing we can say for certain about this table is that there are four columns, two of which are columns of names, and two of which are columns of numbers. We also assume that the whole purpose of organising this information in this way is to emphasise that the data-items are related in some way. The data on its own however conveys little actual information. We cannot interpret it properly until we assign some rudimentary semantics. This we do in the relational data model by assigning a suitable relation name and some suitable names for columns. For example:

Wards

Ward No.	Ward Name	No of Beds	Sister Name
10	Bryn Siriol	6	N. Hughes
12	Cefn Coed	8	T. Evans
15	Merthyr	10	M. Thomas
20	Rhondda	12	G. Jones

The existence of these names would allow most people to interpret this table correctly. Note however, as good database designers, we have chosen deliberately helpful names. This is good practice, but there is no inherent need in the relational data model for mnemonic names (Bowers, 1989). This flexibility has the consequence that nonsense can frequently be retrieved from a relational database. For instance, in the present generation of RDBMS, it is perfectly possible for us to perform a join on a table containing information about shipping with a table containing information about personnel, to give us the result that the manager of public relations whose surname happens to be *Victoria* displaces 50 000 tons !

8.3.2 A Semantic Data Model and DBMS.

Semantic data models are primarily theoretical models much in the sense that the relational data model is theoretical in nature. We discuss first the most prominent of the semantic data models - the Entity-Relationship data model. We then discuss a practical realisation of the Entity-Relationship approach in a DBMS known as GENERIS. GENERIS was originally developed by a number of researchers at the University of Strathclyde and is now marketed by Deductive Systems Ltd.

The Entity-Relationship data model (E-R model) was originally advocated by P.P.S.Chen (Chen, 1976). Intended to be a direct competitor to the Relational data model it is now more commonly used as a conceptual modelling tool for database design. In this sense, the Entity-Relationship model is now more clearly seen as an ally rather than an enemy of the Relational Data Model.

In the E-R model the real world is represented in terms of entities, the relationships between entities and the attributes associated with entities. Entities represent objects of interest in the real world such as *employees*, *departments* and *projects*. Relationships represent named associations between entities. A department *employs* many employees. An employee *is assigned to* a number of projects. *Employs* and *is assigned to* are both relationships in the Entity-Relationship approach. Attributes are properties of an entity or relationship. *Name* is an attribute of the *employee* entity. *Duration of employment* is an attribute of the *employs* relationship.

The original Entity-Relationship model has been extended in a number of ways (Teorey, 1986). One of the most important extensions is the support for generalisation hierarchies (Smith, 1977). This allows us to declare certain entities as instances of other entities. For instance, *manager, secretary* and *technician* might all be declared instances of an *employee* entity. Likewise, *sales managers, production managers* etc. would all be declared instances of the *manager* entity. The important consequence of this facility is that entities lower down in the generalisation hierarchy inherit the attributes of entities higher up. Hence, a *sales manager* would inherit properties of managers in general, and indeed of employees in general.

GENERIS exploits this type of relationship, frequently referred to as a class membership or is-a relationship, throughout the system. In GENERIS such a relationship is referred to as a generic association (Brachman, 1983). Facts can be declared in GENERIS using generic associations. For instance:

> manager is an employee
> sales_manager is a manager

are both valid commands in GENERIS.

Class relationships do not however only relate entities to entities. They are also used to relate entities to attributes and values. For instance, the following facts establish the employee *Allen's* place in the generalisation hierarchy, or perhaps more accurately lattice, of a GENERIS database.

> Allen is an employee
> Allen has age 32
> Allen has department Accounts

This approach has a number of advantages over the relational approach. For example, the relationship between a class and an entity is normally fulfilled via the notion of an explicitly declared index in a conventional relational system. In GENERIS this form of association is created transparently and dynamically whenever facts are inserted into the database.

This also leads to a simplification of queries expressed on an Entity-Relationship database. If we wanted to find the age and department of an employee named *Allen* using SQL we would probably express it as follows:

> SELECT name, department, age
> FROM employees
> WHERE name = 'Allen'

A GENERIS version of the same query would be:

> DISPLAY department and age for Allen

This means that a GENERIS database holds more semantic knowledge than a relational database. GENERIS does not need to be told in which table the data is stored. It does not need to be told that Allen is an employee since it should know that through the generic associations it has stored.

This is what it means to be an implementation of a semantic data model. A GENERIS schema incorporates more knowledge about the real-world domain being modelled than we would find in a relational database.

8.3.3 The Future of Semantic Data Models

It took some several years after Codd's publication of his seminal paper on the relational data model for the first papers on semantic data modelling to appear. I have argued elsewhere (Beynon-Davies, 1990) that this means that implementations of semantic modelling principles are unlikely to overtake relational database systems in the short term. There are also other good reasons for expecting relational systems to continue to be pre-eminent over the next decade. SDMs, for instance, have been heavily criticised by Codd for lacking a clear formal foundation (Codd, 1990). Nevertheless, some reports predict DBMS based on SDM ideas will overtake relational systems in the long term (OVUM, 1988). What will probably happen in practice is that relational products will eventually extend themselves into the semantic modelling arena. There are already signs of this happening (Beynon-Davies, 1990 and Stone-braker, 1984).

8.4 Object-Oriented Database Systems

An OVUM report published in 1989 predicts that database systems adhering to an object-oriented data model as opposed to a relational data model will overtake relational database systems by the mid 1990s (OVUM, 1988). There is no doubt that *object-oriented* is clearly a 'good thing' to be at the time of writing. There is some confusion however about what it actually means to be *object-oriented*. The present section attempts a brief discussion of this issue.

The term object-oriented is used in a number of different senses within contemporary computing. The term was first applied to a group of languages descended from a Scandinavian invention known as SIMULA. SIMULA was the first language to introduce the concept of an abstract data type, an integrated package of data structures and procedures. Probably the best known object-oriented programming language is SMALL-TALK - a programming environment developed at the Xerox Park Research Institute.

It is only comparatively recently that the term object-oriented has been applied to database systems. The main difference between object-oriented programming languages and databases is that object-oriented database systems require the existence of persistent objects. In object-oriented programming languages, objects exist only for the span of program execution. In object-oriented database systems, objects have a life in secondary storage over and above the execution of programs.

There is little agreement also concerning the difference between an object-oriented data model and many of the semantic data models such as the Entity-Relationship data model. Perhaps a possible distinction can be made using a structural/behavioural framework. Semantic data models are usually seen as mechanisms for producing structural abstractions. In contrast, object-oriented data models are geared more towards providing behavioural abstractions. In other words, semantic data models are geared more towards the representation of data while object-oriented data models are geared more towards the manipulation of data (King, 1988).

To manage an object-oriented database we need an object-oriented DBMS. An object-oriented DBMS is a system with the following capabilities (Ullman, 1988):

(1) The ability to define and manipulate complex objects (objects with a nested structure). This issue will be discussed in greater depth in section 8.6.

(2) Inherent in the definition of any object is a set of procedures for manipulating the object. All access to the object is via these in-built procedures. The classic example of an object is a *stack*. The in-built procedures of this object would be *push* and *pop* operations.

(3) Inherent support for object identity. This is the ability to distinguish between two objects with the same characteristics. The relational data model is a value-oriented data model. It does not inherently support the notion of a distinct identifier for each object in the database. Hence, in the relational data model two identical tuples must fundamentally refer to the same object. In an object-oriented database two identical records can refer to two distinct objects via the notion of a unique system-generated identifier.

Object-oriented DBMS is still very much a developing research area. A number have emerged on the commercial arena including Vbase (now re-named as Ontos) from Ontologic Inc. (Navathe, 1989) and Gemstone/Opal from Servologic (Ullman, 1989).

There is still some debate about whether Object-Oriented data-base systems offer a better alternative to database management than relational database systems. Date, for instance, has portrayed ob-ject-oriented DBMS as something of a step-back, at least as far as standard data processing applications are concerned (Date, 1990). His main reservation is that object-oriented database systems demand the detailed specification of data manipulation in procedural terms. This seems to run counter to the non-procedural emphasis of relational data manipulation.

There is no doubt however that an object-oriented approach seems particularly well-suited to certain non-standard applications such as the management of computer graphics. It is to this issue that we now turn.

8.5 Multi-Media Databases

A multi-media database is a repository for different types of media, eg, data, text, sound, graphics etc. Many multi-media database systems use an object-oriented approach as discussed in the previous section. In this section, we examine one such system available on the Apple Macintosh, Hypercard (APPLE, 1987).

Hypercard is both an authoring tool and a *cassette player* for in-formation. As a cassette player the user navigates through a series of non-linear connections between pieces of information. As an authoring tool, Hypercard can be used to create a multi-media database.

The central unit of information in a Hypercard system is the card, which is a screenful of information. It may be a map, a data entry screen or any other screen of information. Cards are normally made up of entities known as fields and buttons. A field is a display area and may correspond to the conventional data processing notion of the term. A button is a navigating mechanism. Buttons are used to provide the necessary inter-connections between cards stored together in units called stacks. A stack in Hypercard is therefore a multi-media database.

The simplest use of Hypercard is in browsing mode. Here, the user navigates through a given stack by using a mouse device to click on a button. Every button may have an associated script, a piece of code written in the Hypercard authoring language, Hypertalk. It is this script which tells the system where to go next. Below, we have one of the simplest forms of script:

```
on mouseUp
    go to next card
end mouseUp
```

It simply tells the system to display the next associated card in the stack when the mouse button is released.

Hypercard is built upon object-oriented principles. While Hypercard is running, the system sends messages to objects in the stack about the current state of the system. For instance, when the mouse button is pressed, a mouseDown message is sent. The receiver of the message depends upon where the browse pointer is located at the time the message is sent. If the object under the pointer contains a message handler - an associated script for the message - then the actions specified in the handler are executed. If there is no such message handler then the message is passed upwards through the Hypercard hierarchy (see figure 8.2) to the stack level, and so on.

Hypercard can be used in association with a conventional RDBMS such as ORACLE. This allows application-builders the attractive pos-

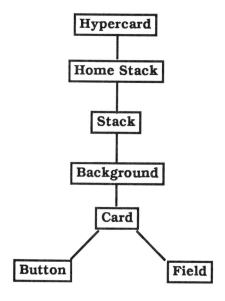

Figure 8.2

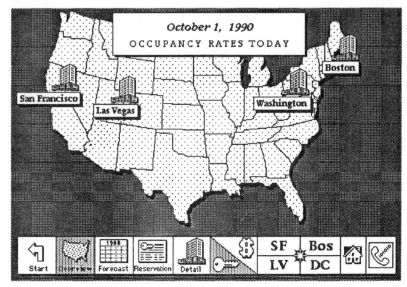

Figure 8.3

sibility of creating visual interfaces to data contained in relational databases. One example known to the author, for instance, simulates a distributed database system for hotel administration. On startup the user can gain an overview of the hotels owned by the company by clicking on the overview button. A map of the United States is then displayed with

Figure 8.4

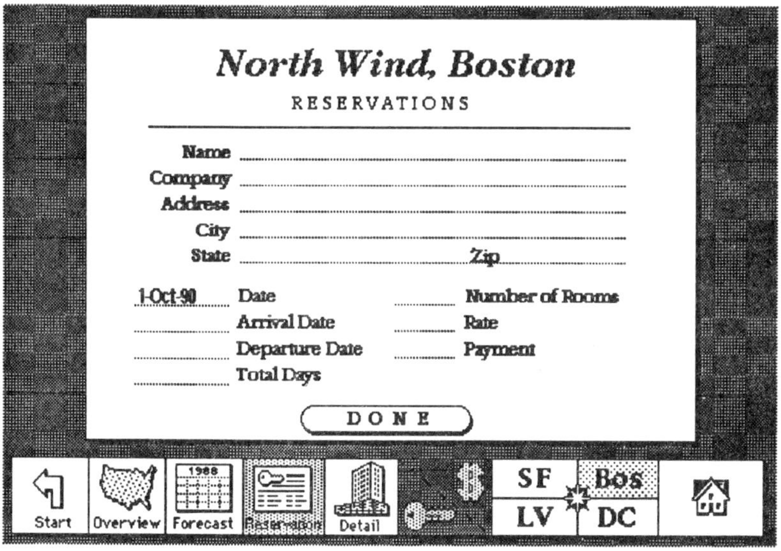

Figure 8.5

icons for the four hotels run by the company located over major cities (see figure 8.3). To book a reservation at one of these hotels we click on the reservations button. We then select the hotel we are interested in (figure 8.4) and fill in the relevant details of our stay on the card displayed. Assuming the details entered pass the validation rules established for the application, a series of entries are made to the underlying ORACLE database (see figure 8.5).

8.6 Extending the Relational Data Model

Because of the mathematical simplicity of their underlying data model, relational databases have proven to be extremely successful at supporting standard data processing applications such as accounting, payroll and personnel. A number of emerging non-standard applications in areas such as office automation, knowledgebase systems and computer aided design however have caused many people to reassess the position of the relational data model for database management. Such non-standard applications demand the support of complex objects such as documents, rules and graphics. Although powerful, the relational data model is generally considered insufficient for supporting this new *object-orientation*.

Two alternative approaches to object-orientation have been proposed.

The first is to replace the relational data model with a semantically richer data model more clearly suited to the needs of object-orientation. Hence, as we discussed in section 8.3, much work has gone into developing DBMS based on semantic data models such as the Entity-Relationship approach. The second alternative is to exploit the capabilities of the relational model and to extend them into the object-oriented domain. It is this latter approach we consider in this section. Specifically we consider how the concept of an Abstract Data Type (ADT) can be added to the relational model to improve its object orientation (Osborn, 1986).

8.6.1 Abstract Data Types

Most existing relational database systems provide only a limited number of data types for the user. For example, SQL-based systems provide *integer, character, date, real* data types, etc. These are usually sufficient for most standard data processing applications. For other applications, such as office automation however, these data types are not sufficiently rich. An office automation system, for instance, might want a document data type. One solution to this problem is to extend the range of primitive data types offered to the user by the DBMS. The vast number of data types needed to support the infiltration of computing into more and more areas is probably too large however to make this a practicable solution. A better approach is therefore to make the DBMS infinitely extendable by the user through user-defined and implemented Abstract Data Types.

An abstract data type or ADT is a type of object that defines a domain of values and a set of operations designed to work with these values. The objective of an ADT is to provide a characteristic known as *information hiding*. Implementation details of the ADT are hidden from higher levels of an application system. If the implementation of an ADT is changed, the upper layers of a system are unaffected since they communicate with the ADT only through a set of abstract operations composing its interface.

Suppose we have a system designed to store the written materials of a consultant psychiatrist. In our psychiatric documentation system a *note* might be a new ADT defined by the system designer. A create statement in SQL might exploit this ADT as follows:

```
CREATE TABLE consultations
    (nhs_no CHAR(10) NOT NULL,
     appointment DATE NOT NULL,
     consult_record NOTE NOT NULL)
```

Associated with this new data type might be the operation *count._note*. This would count the number of words in a consultation note. Assuming that the number of words per consultation would give the psychiatrist some idea of the importance of the record, the following SQL query might prove useful:

```
SELECT nhs_no
FROM consultations
WHERE appointment > '30-JUN-90'
ORDER BY COUNT_NOTE(consult_record) DESC
```

This query would extract the NHS numbers of patients seen after the 30th of June 1990 and order the results in descending order of the size of their consultation record.

ADTs can be used to model not only new atomic objects but also complex objects. A complex object can be defined as an object having a hierarchical structure whose attributes can be atomic or indeed complex objects themselves. To continue with the psychiatry example, suppose that *history* was an ADT declared to the system. *History* might be composed not only of the total number of consultations relevant to a given patient but such patient details as name, age, address etc. In this context a count operation would have a different interpretation. If we declared *patient_record* to be an attribute of type *history, count(patient_record)* might tell us the number of consultations that a patient has had.

8.7 Conclusion: From Database through InformationBase to KnowledgeBase

In this chapter we have established that the concept of a database system is not a static entity. It is a fluid concept evolving in nature as more and more areas are demanding mass information storage.

In many senses the term database system may be an inadequate one for the newer types of proposals being put forward. Data is a collection of isolated facts. In our *employees* file, for instance, we store facts such as *Allen is a salesman* or *Smith is a clerk*. Hence, a database, being a collection of such files, is a mechanism for storing a large collection of isolated facts.

A database based on a semantic data model such as the E-R model however contains more than simply an isolated collection of facts. It contains some representation of meaningful relationships holding between objects in the database. We store, for instance in an Entity-Relationship database such as GENERIS a class relationship such as *a manager is an employee*. Hence, it is probably more accurate to call such a system an informationbase system. There are more semantics built into such a system.

Even this definition is not enough, however, for many people. They want systems to handle knowledge. Knowledge in computational terms might be defined as a combination of facts and rules. Facts are the traditional stuff of database systems. Rules have emerged in work done in areas such as expert systems. Rules have a place in the database arena particularly in the area of database integrity. As we discussed in chapter 4, for instance, an integrity constraint such as *no employee should earn more than his manager* is a rule. Hence, researchers are proposing systems to handle an amalgam of factbases and rulebases. They are

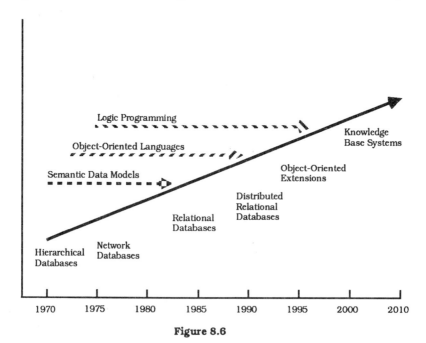

Figure 8.6

proposing knowledgebase systems.

The search is on for an appropriate architecture for such knowledgebase systems. One group of people see hope in an approach such as the Object-Oriented paradigm. Another group of people are attempting to build upon the strong theoretical foundation of the Relational data model. One interesting area because it fits well with the mathematical rigour of relational databases is the idea of using logic to build knowledgebase systems (Gallaire, 1978). That field however needs another book to itself. Figure 8.3 plots some of the developments discussed in this chapter against a probable time-scale of events.

8.8 Exercises

(1) What sort of facilities are likely to be in the SQL2 standard that are not in the existing SQL standard?
(2) What advantages arise from having a standard for SQL?
(3) Why is the relational data model regarded as being semantically weak?
(4) Describe the main properties of a semantic data model.
(5) Describe the main properties of an object-oriented database system.
(6) Distinguish between a semantic data model and an object-oriented data model.
(7) What is a multi-media database?
(8) What is an Abstract Data Type?
(9) Why do you think the storage and manipulation of text is best handled by an object-oriented as opposed to a relational approach?
(10) What advantages do you think arise from extending the relational data model as opposed to replacing it with another data model?
(11) Define knowledge in computational terms.

Glossary

Abstract Data Type (ADT)
A programming abstraction. A package of data structures and procedures.

Abstraction
The process of modelling 'real-world' concepts in a computational medium.

Accommodation
The process of producing a relational schema from a dependency diagram or entity-relationship diagram.

Additional Integrity
Business rules of some enterprise. A business rule such as when a foreign key can be null or not in a table (see Referential Integrity).

Ad-hoc Query
An information retrieval request not pre-planned and stored in a database system.

ANSI
American National Standards Institute. A group of representatives from organisations belonging to the Computer and Business Equipment Manufacturing Association. ANSI forms special committees to develop standards for various areas of computing.

Attribute
A column in a relation.

Cardinality
The number of columns or attributes in a relation.

CASE
Computer Aided/Assisted Software Engineering. Tools devoted to automating various stages of information systems development.

Clustering
The process of storing logically related records close together on some secondary storage device.

CODASYL
Conference on Data Systems Languages. A body that developed the COBOL language and specified the network data model.

Column
See Attribute.

Concurrency
The simultaneous access to a database by more than one user.

Consistency
The process of ensuring that a set of related actions are performed together or not at all.

Cursor
An embedded SQL construct used to interface SQL's *multiple-record-at-a-time* way of working with 3GL's *single-record-at-a-time* way of working.

Data Analysis
The process of producing a database design.

Database
A structured pool of organisational data.

Database Administrator (DBA)
Person given the overall responsibility for controlling a particular database system.

Database Management System (DBMS)
A system which manages all interactions with a database.

Database System
A system composed of a database and database management system.

Data Control Language (DCL)

That part of a data model concerned with controlling database use.

Data Definition Language (DDL)

That part of a data model concerned with defining data structures.

Data Dictionary

A concept either used to represent the system tables of a relational database or a more encompassing representation of the data used by some enterprise.

Data Manipulation Language (DML)

That part of a data model concerned with maintaining data in a database and retrieving information from the database.

Data Model

An architecture for data. Comprises three primary components: data structures, data operators and inherent integrity rules.

Data Type

A definition of the type of data that can be stored in the columns of a table.

Degree

The number of rows or tuples in a relation.

Dependency

An association between data items. Data item B is said to be dependent on data item A if, whenever a value for data item A appears, one unambiguous value for data item B appears.

Dependency Diagram

See Determinancy Diagram.

Dependent Data Item

A data item whose values are determined by another data item.

Determinancy

The opposite of dependency.

Determinancy Diagram

A diagram which documents the determinant or dependent relationships between data items relevant to some application.

Determinant

A data item which determines the values of another data item.

Difference

An operator of the Relational Algebra. A commutative operator which produces from two tables a table of the rows not common to both tables.

Divide

An operator of the Relational Algebra. Divide takes two tables as input and produces one table as output. One of the input tables must be a binary table, i.e., it must have two columns. The other input table must be a unary table, a one column table. The unary table must also be defined on the same domain as one of the columns of the binary table.

Domain

The pool of values that may be assigned to an attribute or column.

Entity

Some aspect of the real world which has an independent existence and can be uniquely identified.

Entity Integrity

An inherent integrity rule of the relational data model. Every table or relation must have a primary key.

Entity-Relationship Model

A data model due to P.P.S Chen which models data in terms of entities and relationships.

Field

A portion of a record containing some value.

File

A collection of data stored on some secondary storage device.

Foreign Key
An attribute of a relation which references the primary key of some other relation.

HYPERCARD
A multi-media system available on the APPLE Macintosh.

Index
A file of pointers connecting logical values with physical storage locations.

Inherent Integrity
The integrity rules built into the data model as architecture. Entity and referential integrity are the inherent integrity rules of the relational data model.

Integrity
Maintaining the logical consistency of a database.

Integrity Constraint
A rule for maintaining integrity.

Intersection
An operator of the Relational Algebra. Intersection is fundamentally the opposite of union. Whereas union produces the combination of two sets or tables, intersection produces a result table which contains rows common to both input tables.

IRDS
Information Resource Dictionary System. A repository or record of all the information resources used by some organisation.

Join
An operator of the Relational Algebra. The join operator takes two relations as input and produces one relation as output.

Key
That part of a file primarily used to access records.

Lock
A mechanism used to temporarily shut out users from data access.

Multi-Media Database
A database storing various different media, e.g. data, text, sound, images etc.

Non-Procedural Query Language
A query language in which the user can specify what is required and leave it up to the DBMS to sort out the procedural details.

Normalisation
The process of transforming a data set subject to a whole range of update anomalies into a data set free from such anomalies.

Object-Oriented Database
A database system founded on an object-oriented data model.

Primary Key
The identifier for each tuple in a relation.

Program-Data Independence
The immunity of applications to changes in the underlying structure of a database and vice versa.

Project
An operator of the Relational Algebra. Produces a subset of the columns of a table.

Query Optimisation
The process of transforming a query expressed in non-procedural terms into a query expressed in procedural terms.

Record
A portion of a file representing properties of a single entity.

Referential Integrity
An inherent integrity constraint of the Relational Data Model. A foreign key value must either be null or a value of the primary key of a related table.

Relation
The fundamental data structure of the Relational Data Model. A disciplined table.

Relational Algebra
The manipulative part of the Relational Data Model.

Relational Calculus
An alternative to the Relational Algebra as the manipulative part of the Relational Data Model.

Relational Data Model
A data model originally created by E.F.Codd.

Report
A formatted listing of some extract of a database.

Report Generator
A piece of software used for the production of reports from a database.

Row
See Tuple.

Schema
A representation of the structure of some database.

Select
An operator of the Relational Algebra. Produces a subset of the rows of a table.

Semantic Data Model (SDM)
A data model having a richer set of constructs for modelling the real world than the Relational Data Model.

SEQUEL
See SQL.

Structured Query Language (SQL)
A database sub-language emerging as the standard interface to relational systems.

Sub-query
An embedded query within a SQL select statement.

Table
See Relation.

Transaction
A logical unit of work.

Trigger
An active integrity constraint causing changes to be made to the state of some database when a given condition is met.

Tuple
A row in a relation.

Union
An operator of the Relational Algebra. Union is an operator which takes two compatible relations as input and produces one relation as output.

View
A virtual table. A window into a database.

View Integration
A lateral approach to data analysis.

References and Further Reading

ANSI (1986) Database Language SQL. ANSI X3.135-1986.

ANSI (1989a) Database Language SQL Addendum 1. ANSI X3.135.1-1989.

ANSI (1989b) Database Language SQL2 (Working Draft). ANSI X3H2-89-259.

ANSI (1989c) Information Resource Dictionary Systems. ANSI X3.138-1989.

APPLE (1987). Hypercard User's Guide. Cupertino, California.

Beech David. (1989) New Life for SQL. Datamation. Feb. 1989. pp. 29-36.

Beynon-Davies Paul. (1987) Software Engineering and Knowledge Engineering: Unhappy Bedfellows. Computer Bulletin. Dec. 1987.

Beynon-Davies Paul. (1989) Information Systems Development. Macmillan. London.

Beynon-Davies Paul. (1990) Expert Database Systems: A Gentle Introduction. Mcgraw-Hill. London.

Bing Yao S. (ed.). (1985) Principles of Database Design. Vol 1: Logical Organisations. Prentice-Hall. Englewood Cliffs. N.J.

Bowers David S. (1989) From Database to Information Base: Some Questions of Semantics and Constraints. Information and Software Technology.

Brachman R.J. (1983) What IS-A is and isn't: an Analysis of the Taxonomic Links in Semantic Networks. Computer. October. 1983. pp 30-36.

Brodie Michael L. (1984) On the Development of Data Models. In Brodie, 84.

Brodie Michael.L. and Mylopoulos J. (eds). (1984) On Conceptual Modelling. Springer-Verlag. New York.

Ceri Stefano and Pelagatti Giuseppe. (1984) Distributed Databases: Principles and Systems. Mcgraw-Hill. New York.

Chen Peter Pin-Shan. (1976) The Entity-Relationship Model - Toward a Unified View of Data. ACM Transactions on Database Systems. Vol. 1. No. 1. March 1976. pp. 9-36.

Codd E.F. (1970) A Relational Model for Large Shared Data Banks. Communications of ACM. Vol. 13. No. 6. June 1970. pp 377 - 387.

Codd E.F. (1979) Extending the Relational Database Model to Capture More Meaning. ACM Transactions on Database Systems. Vol. 4. No. 4. Dec. 1979. pp 397-434.

Codd E.F. (1982) Relational Database: A Practical Foundation for Productivity. Comm. ACM. Vol. 25. No. 2.

Codd E.F. (1985) Is Your Relational Database Management System Really Relational? An Evaluation Scheme. Keynote speech presented at ORACLE user's conference. August 1985.

Codd E.F. (1988a) Fatal Flaws in SQL. Datamation. Aug 1988. pp. 45-48.

Codd E.F. (1988b) Fatal Flaws in SQL. Part 2. Datamation. Sept 1988. pp. 71-74.

Codd E.F. (1990) The Relational Model for Database Management: Version 2. Addison-Wesley. Reading, Mass.

Date C.J. (1987) Where SQL Falls Short. Datamation. May 1987. pp. 83-86.

Date C.J. (1989). A Guide to the SQL Standard (2nd ed.). Addison-Wesley. Reading, Mass.

Date C.J. (1990) An Introduction to Databases Systems. Vol. 1. 5th ed. Addison-Wesley. Reading, Mass.

Dolk Daniel.R. and Kirsch Robert A. (1987) A Relational Information Resource Dictionary System. Comm. of ACM. Jan. 1987. Vol 30. No. 1.

Dutka Alan F. and Hanson Howard H. (1989) Fundamentals of Data Normalisation. Addison-Wesley. Reading, Mass.

Elmasri Ramez and Navathe Shamkant B. (1989) Fundamentals of Database Systems. Benjamin Cummings. Redwood City, California.

Frost R.A. (1982) Binary-Relational Storage Structures. The Computer Journal. Vol. 25. No. 3. pp 358-367.

Frost R.A. (1983) SCHEMAL: Yet Another Conceptual Schema Definition Language. The Computer Journal. Vol. 26. No. 3.

Furtado A.E. and Neuhold E.J. (1986) Formal Techniques for Database Design. Springer-Verlag. Berlin. 1986.

Gallaire H. and Minker G. (1978) (eds). Logic and Databases. Plenum Press.

Gardarin G. and Gellenbe E. (1984) New Applications of Database Systems. Academic Press. London.

Goldfine A. (1985) The Information Resource Dictionary System. Proc. 4th Entity-Relationship Conf. IEEE Press. pp 114-122.

Gray Peter. (1985) Logic, Algebra, and Databases. Ellis-Horwood. Chichester. 1985.

Howe D.R. (1983) Data Analysis for Data Base Design. Edward Arnold. London.

ISO (1987). Information Processing Systems - Database Language SQL. ISO/TC97/SC21/WG3 N117.

ISO (1989). Database Language SQL with Integrity Enhancement. ISO/IEC 9075.

Jarke Mathias and Koch J. (1984) Query Optimisation in Database Systems. Computer Surveys. Vol. 16. No. 2. pp 112-152.

Kerschberg L. (1987) Expert Database Systems. Computer Bulletin. June 1987.

Kim Won and Lochovsky Fred. (1988) Object-Oriented Languages, Applications and Databases. Addison-Wesley. Reading, Mass.

King Roger. (1988) My Cat is Object-Oriented. In Kim, 1988.

King Roger and Mcleod Dennis. (1985) Semantic Data Models. In Bing Yao (1985).

Kowalski Robert. (1979a) Algorithm = Logic + Control. Comm. of ACM. Vol . 22. No. 7.

Kowalski Robert. (1979b) Logic for Problem Solving. North Holland. Amsterdam.

Lloyd J.W. (1983) An Introduction to Deductive Database Systems. The Australian Computer Journal. Vol. 15. No. 2. May 1983. pp 52-57

Martin J. (1984) An Information Systems Development Manifesto. Prentice-Hall. Englewood Cliffs N.J.

Morgenstern M. (1983) Active Databases as a Paradigm for Enhanced Computing Environments. 9th Int. VLDB Conf. Florence. pp 34-42.

Mylopoulos John and Brodie Michael. (1989) Readings in Artificial Intelligence and Databases. Morgan Kaufmann. New York.

Navathe Shamkant B. and Kerschberg Larry. (1986) The Role of Data Dictionaries in Information Resource Management. Information and Management. Vol. 10. pp 21-46. North Holland.

ORACLE (1987a) SQL*Plus Users Guide. Version 2.0. Belmont, California.

ORACLE (1987b) Database Administrator's Guide. Version 5.1. Belmont, California.

ORACLE (1987c) SQL*Forms Users Guide. Belmont, California.

Osborn Sylvia L. and Heaven T.E. (1986) The Design of a Relational Database System with Abstract Data Types for Domains. ACM Trans on Database Systems. Vol. 11. No. 3. Sept. 1986. pp 357-373.

OVUM Report. (1988) The Future of Databases. OVUM Press. London.

Peckham Joan and Maryanski Fred. (1988) Semantic Data Models. ACM Computing Surveys. Vol. 20, No. 3, Sept. pp 153-189.

Smith John Miles and Smith Diane C.P. (1977) Database Abstractions: Aggregation and Generalisation. ACM.

Stonebraker Michael. (1984) Adding Semantic Knowledge to a Relational Database System. In Brodie, 1984.

Stonebraker Michael (ed). (1986) The INGRES Papers. Addison-Wesley. Reading, Mass.

Storey Veda C. and Goldstein Robert C. (1988) A Methodology for Creating User Views in Database Design. ACM Transactions on Database Systems. Vol. 13. No. 3. Sept. 1988. pp. 305-338.

Teorey T. J., Yang D., Fry J.P. (1986) A Logical Design Methodology for Relational Databases Using the Extended Entity-Relationaship Model. ACM Computing Surveys. 18. 2. June. 1986. pp. 197-222.

Tsitchizris D.C and Lochovsky F.J. (1982) Data Models. Prentice-Hall. Englewood Cliffs, N.J.

Ullman Jeffrey D. (1988) Principles of Database and Knowledge-base Systems. Vol. 1. Computer Science Press. Rockville, Maryland.

Ullman Jeffrey D. (1989) Principles of Database and Knowledge-base Systems. Vol. 2. Computer Science Press. Rockville, Maryland.

Wiederhold G. (1984) Knowledge and Database Management. IEEE Software. Jan. 1984. pp 63-73.

Wiorkowski G. and Kull D. (1988) DB2 Design and Development Guide. Addison-Wesley. Reading, Mass.

Suggested Solutions

Chapter 1. Databases, Data Models and Database Management Systems

(1) Data sharing, integration, independence, integrity, security, abstraction.

(2) A filing cabinet is an organised information repository. A file in a cabinet is analogous to a file in a database. A card in a filing cabinet is analogous to a record in a database file, etc.

(3) The ability to add new files to a database, remove files from a database, restrict access to files in a database , insert new data into existing files, update data in existing files, delete data from existing files, retrieve data from existing files.

(4) The term, data model, is used to describe an architecture for data as in the relational data model. It is also used to describe the rules of some business application as in the rules of an order entry system.

(5) A set of data structures, a set of data operators, a set of inherent integrity rules.

(6) The relational data model consists of one data structure, the relation, nine fundamental operators, packaged as the relational algebra, and two inherent integrity rules, entity and referential integrity.

(7) It can act as a standard language for people using relational database systems, allowing easy migration from one RDBMS to another. It also encourages communication not only between database and database but also between database systems and CASE tools.

Chapter 2. Data Definition

(1) Relations are a subset of the domain of discourse defined by the concept of a table. A relation is a table that obeys a restricted set of rules.

(2) The table contains repeating groups, i.e., the patient data for each ward.

(3) A primary key is a column or set of columns of a table chosen to uniquely identify rows of the table.

(4) A foreign key is a column or set of columns of a table which is also the primary key of some other table in a database.

(5) A domain is a set of values defined over a column of a table.

(6) A non-meaningful serial number.

(7) They define the structure of the underlying database. In this sense, they are frequently referred to as a meta-database.

(8) CREATE TABLE departments
     (deptno NUMBER(2),
     name CHAR(20),
     loc CHAR(20))

(9) CREATE TABLE departments
     (deptno NUMBER(2) NOT NULL,
     name CHAR(20),
     loc CHAR(10))
     CREATE UNIQUE INDEX dept_ind ON
     departments(deptno)

(10) ALTER TABLE departments
     MODIFY (loc char(20))

(11) CREATE INDEX loc_ind ON
     departments(loc)

(12) DROP INDEX loc_ind

(13) DROP TABLE departments

(14) Cardinality.

Chapter 3. Data Manipulation

(1) Data manipulation has four aspects: inputting data, removing data, amending data and retrieving data.

(2) Each operator takes one or more relations as input and produces one relation as output.

(3) Difference.

(4) (a) SELECT employees WHERE ename = 'Allen' -> T1
   (b) PROJECT departments(deptno) ->T1
   (c) SELECT employees WHERE empno = 7788 -> T1
      PROJECT T1(ename) ->T2
   (d) JOIN employees WITH departments ON deptno
      WHERE dname = 'Research' -> T1
      PROJECT T1(ename) -> T2

(5) Sub-queries.

(6) In the relational algebra a query is a series of steps with intermediate results. In SQL a query is one statement with one final result.

(7) (a) SELECT *
         FROM employees
         WHERE ename = 'Jones'

   (b) SELECT deptno
        FROM departments

   (c) SELECT ename
        FROM employees
        WHERE empno = 7788

   (d) SELECT ename
        FROM employees
        WHERE deptno =   (SELECT deptno
                            FROM departments
                            WHERE dname = 'Research')

(8)   SELECT AVG(salary)
       FROM employees
       WHERE deptno =   (SELECT deptno
                        FROM departments
                        WHERE dname = 'Accounts')

(9) (a) CREATE TABLE managers
         (mgrno number(4) NOT NULL,
         name char(10),
         salary number(7,2),
         start date,
         dept number(2))
         INSERT INTO
         managers(number,name,salary,start,dept)
         SELECT empno,ename,salary,hiredate,deptno
         FROM employees
         WHERE job = 'Manager'
         DELETE FROM employees
         WHERE job = 'Manager'

   (b) UPDATE EMPLOYEES
        SET salary = salary * 1.15
        WHERE job ='Salesman'

Chapter 4. Data Integrity

(1)   There is a close correspondence between the facts stored in the
       database and the real world it models.

(2) Relational products have been traditionally poor at supporting integrity mechanisms. Further development is needed.

(3) Inherent integrity is integrity as defined by the relational data model. Additional integrity is integrity as defined by the business data model.

(4) Every table must have a primary key.

(5) If a table has a foreign key then values of that foreign key must either refer to a primary key value elsewhere in the database or be null.

(6) It depends on the rules of the business as defined by a particular application.

(7) (a) Restricted Delete means we forbid the deletion of a row from the primary table until all associated rows within the foreign table have been deleted.

   (b) Cascades Delete means if we delete a primary row then all associated foreign rows are deleted.

   (c) Nullifies Delete means that if we delete a primary row then we must set the foreign key values to null.

(8) Restricted Delete because only checking is involved. No chain of updates are needed.

(9) Via creating a unique index on a column delared as NOT NULL.

(10) Because a major part of any traditional data processing application is made up of data integrity.

(11) An assertion is simply a rule expressed on a database. Assertions are passive integrity mechanisms. They are created merely to prohibit certain states of a database from occurring. Triggers are active integrity mechanisms. They are used to propagate a string of associated updates throughout the database. An alerter is a variant of the trigger mechanism. Rather than causing changes of the database to occur, however, an alerter notifies specific users of happenings in the database.

(12) Easier communication between database systems, CASE tools and information systems created using such tools.

Chapter 5. Data Control

(1) Data control is the activity which concerns itself with allocating access to data and allocating access to facilities for manipulating data. Data control is normally the responsibility of the DBA.

(2) A view is a virtual table. It has no actual existence. It merely acts in the capacity of a window onto base tables.

(3) To simplify, to provide security and to provide functionality.

(4) Because in some views particular updates are ambiguous, as in the case of a view without a primary key.

(5) In the main, views comprising a select from one table.

(6) CREATE VIEW allen AS
SELECT empno, ename
FROM employees
WHERE deptno =   (SELECT deptno
                             FROM employees
                             WHERE ename = 'Allen')

(7) CREATE VIEW london AS
SELECT empno, ename
FROM employees E, departments D
WHERE E.deptno = D.deptno
AND loc = 'London'

(8) CREATE VIEW retirement AS
SELECT empno, ename
FROM employees
WHERE (65 - age) <= 5

(9) CREATE VIEW managers AS
SELECT *
FROM employees
WHERE job = 'Manager'
GRANT ALL ON managers TO king

(10) CREATE VIEW london AS
SELECT *
FROM employees E, departments D
WHERE E.deptno = D.deptno
AND loc = 'London'
GRANT SELECT ON london TO miller

Chapter 6. Data Analysis

(1) Data analysis is the process of building a business data model and representing it as a relational schema. Data analysis is also referred to as logical database design.

(2) Bottom-up data analysis must have a pool of data items, extracted probably from an examination of existing enterprise documentation.

To this pool of data items we apply a series of transformation rules. Bottom-up data analysis is also called normalisation.

(3) A normalised database is relatively free from file maintenance anomalies.

(4) The step-by-step approach is particularly difficult to perform systematically in practice on large data sets. A diagramming approach permits an easier, incremental approach to normalisation.

(5) Data-item B is said to be functionally dependent on data-item A if for every value of A there is one, unambiguous value for B. Data-item B is said to be non-functionally dependent on data-item A if for every value of data-item A there is a delimited set of values for data-item B.

(6) Accommodation is the process of transforming a determinancy diagram into a relational schema.

(7) Students(student-id, student_name)
Lecturers(lecturer-id, lecturer_name)
Courses(course-id, course_name)
Grades(course-id, student-id, grade)

(8) Dependents(employee-no, dependent_name, dependent_DOB)
Employees(employee-no, employee_name, department_code)
Departments(department-code, department_name, department_location)
Emp_Skills(employee-no, skill_code, skill_level)
Skills(skill-code, skill_name, skill_where_obtained)

Chapter 7. Application Development

(1) The DBMS kernel represents most of the database management functions discussed in this book under the headings data definition, data manipulation, data integrity and data control. A database toolkit represents a range of other software products, sometimes supplied by third party vendors, such as spreadsheets and application development tools which interface to the database via the kernel.

(2) Interpreted SQL is interactive. The user types in a statement and receives a response, types in another statement and receives another response. Embedded SQL is designed for use with a host language such as COBOL or C. The SQL statements are usually subject to pre-compilation in this form.

(3) Primarily for use by application developers with experience of host

language use.

(4) The mismatch between SQL's file-at-a-time way of working and most 3GL's record-at-time way of working.

(5) A query packaged with formatting statements.

(6) Menus, data entry/retrieval screens, reports.

(7) Faster development time.

Chapter 8. The Future of Relational Database Systems

(1) A create domain statement, facilities for directly handling entity and referential integrity, and a create assertion statement, amongst others.

(2) Reduced retraining costs, application portability, application longevity, better communication between applications.

(3) Because it is purposely designed to be a minimal data model. It does not have a range of facilities for handling issues such as abstraction.

(4) A semantic data model offers a range of constructs for the more effective modelling of semantics. In this respect, people frequently believe SDMs display a greater economy of expression than the relational model.

(5) A collection of persistent complex objects composed of packages of data and procedures which demonstrate information hiding.

(6) A semantic data model is normally used to create structural abstractions. Object-oriented systems are primarily directed at creating behavioural abstractions.

(7) A database composed of different types of media.

(8) A programming abstraction. A package of data structures and procedures.

(9) A cell in a relation is normally designed to hold a single value. Text is composed of a long string of values. Some systems allow the user to store a pointer in a cell to a package of text. This is sufficient from the point of view of storage. It is unsatisfactory however when we want to perform manipulation on text objects.

(10) The relational data model has a firm theoretical foundation based on logic. Any extensions to the relational model must demonstrate a similar logical or formal foundation.

(11) Knowledge in computational terms is made up of facts and rules.

Appendix 1
The Performance of Relational Database Systems

A1.1 The Performance Issue

When RDBMS products first emerged onto the market they were heavily criticised for being poor performers. The relational data model was attacked not only on its ability to support transaction-processing type applications but also in the area of decision support, where relational databases were traditionally held to be strongest.

Since the early years relational DBMS products have proven better and better performance tools. Even so, many organisations using relational technology still find performance a problem. This section examines the performance issue and makes some general suggestions as to how performance can be improved in a relational environment.

A1.2 Logical and Physical Design

With the rise of the relational data model the emphasis in the database literature has changed. The emphasis has moved from a detailed concern with the physical implementation of database systems towards logical database design.

The relational data model is a logical data model. It is an abstract machine devoid of concerns such as how data is stored on some secondary storage device. Codd, for instance, in his publications on the relational data model says little about performance. Performance is of relevance to the idea of physical database design and the architecture of relational database products.

A1.3 Physical Database Design

In chapter 6 we discussed logical database design. The aim of logical database design is to develop a model of enterprise data in abstract terms. Physical database design, in contrast, is the process of implementing a particular business data model in a particular DBMS to meet the performance objectives of some application. To perform physical database design there must therefore be three prerequisites. First, we must have a detailed business data model. Second, we must have a clear idea of the performance objectives of our application. Third, we must have a detailed understanding of the architecture of our chosen DBMS.

The second prerequisite in particular is not easy to achieve. Performance is frequently a balancing act. For instance, by setting fast access to data as a priority we may have to sacrifice a certain amount of speed in terms of data entry. Or, by transforming our database structure to suit the needs of fast access we may have to sacrifice some of the demands of a clean-cut business data model.

A1.4 Selecting a DBMS

The DBMS product you choose for your site can have a marked effect on performance. Some DBMS products, for instance, are closely coupled to their underlying operating systems. Hence they improve performance by exploiting underlying operating system primitives. Other products are loosely coupled with operating systems. They are designed to be more portable, but consequently they may not be as good performers as closely-coupled systems.

Another way in which product selection affects performance is in the area of compiled vs interpreted queries. Some systems compile all the queries run on a database and store for re-use the access plans produced by the optimiser (see section 3.3.10). Other systems interpret queries at run time. As a general rule, compiled queries execute faster than interpreted queries. If your database system is relatively volatile however in the sense that the underlying database undergoes frequent re-structuring or the major accessing of the database is of an adhoc nature then an interpreted approach is probably best.

A1.5 Exploiting the Architecture of a DBMS

Clearly the question of implementing a data model in the best way will depend on the DBMS you are using. In this section we shall discuss some general points that apply to most existing RDBMS.

A1.5.1 Indexing

As we discussed in chapter 4 we should always index on primary and foreign keys. This is because most of the logical accessing of data should occur via primary and foreign keys. Joins, for instance, will dramatically improve in performance with appropriate indexing here. Indexes should also be placed on items regularly retrieved from your database. If you do regular searches on the salary column of the employees file, for instance, then an index should be placed on this column.

An index is however an extra file in your system. The more indexes you have the more space is taken up on disk. If storage is a problem you may have to sacrifice some indexing. An index also takes some time to update. Every time a change is made to the data contained in some table, all relevant indexes have to be updated. The more indexes you have on this table the longer such an update is going to take.

A1.5.2 Clustering

At first sight, clustering seems to violate one of the principle tenets of the relational data model. Namely, that a table should not contain duplicate rows. A cluster is basically a set of tables which, for reasons of retrieval performance, are located contiguously on disk. The table below, for instance, is a clustered version of the employees and departments tables with which we are familiar.

EMPLOYEES

Empno	Ename	Job	Mgr	Hiredate	Salary	Comm	Deptno
7369	Smith	Clerk	7902	17-DEC-80	800		20
20	Research	Bristol					
7499	Allen	Salesman	7698	20-FEB-81	1600	300	30
30	Sales	London					
7521	Ward	Salesman	7698	22-FEB-81	1250	300	30
30	Sales	London					
7566	Jones	Manager	7839	02-APR-81	2975		20
20	Research	Bristol					
7654	Martin	Salesman	7698	28-SEP-81	1250		30
30	Sales	London					
7698	Blake	Manager	7839	01-MAY-81	2850		30
30	Sales	London					
7782	Clarke	Manager	7839	09-JUN-81	2450		10
10	Accounting	London					
7788	Scott	Analyst	7566	09-NOV-81	3000		20
20	Research	Bristol					
7839	King	President		17-NOV-81	5000		10
10	Accounting	London					
7844	Turner	Salesman	7698	08-SEP-81	1500	0	30
30	Sales	London					

etc.

The rationale for clustering departments data with employees data in this way is to improve the joining of employee records with department records. It must be remembered however that clustering, like indexing, is a physical concern. All that matters in terms of the data model is that the user perceives the data as being organised in relational terms. How the data is stored on disk is outside the domain of the data model.

A1.5.3 De-Normalisation

A fully normalised database is often treated as a totem in database circles. The trouble with a fully normalised database however is that they are frequently made up of lot and lots of files. Such files have to be re-constituted via expensive join activities in most of the useful enterprise queries. One way of improving performance is thus to step back from a fully normalised database. In other words, we reintroduce controlled redundancy into our database. Certain parts of the application will then have a boosted retrieval performance at the expense of the need for more complex integrity maintenance.

A1.5.4 Understanding Your Query Optimiser

As we discussed in chapter three, the engine having the greatest effect on retrieval performance is the query optimiser. Each query optimiser for each RDBMS works differently. The same approximate query expressed in SQL, for instance, may run very quickly on one RDBMS but very slowly on another. Understanding as much as possible about the workings of your relevant optimiser is thus essential for good physical database design in relational terms. Unfortunately, many optimisers are transparent products, hidden from the eyes of application developers. Some products, e.g. DB2 have verbs such as *explain* which divulge something of the way in which the optimiser works on a particular query.

Appendix 2
Summary of ORACLE/SQL

Outlined below is a formal definition of SQL syntax. One should note that this is not a complete specification for SQL under ORACLE, but the definition covers all of the syntax used in this book. The syntax symbols used are as follows:

A ::- B   The symbol to the left is defined in terms of the symbols to the right

[A]   A is optional

< A >   A is a literal

< A >,... An iteration of literals

A,...   An iteration of symbols

A : B   Selection. A or B

CREATE-INDEX-statement ::=
    CREATE [UNIQUE] INDEX <index name>
    ON <table name> (<column name>)

CREATE-TABLE-statement ::=
    CREATE TABLE <table name> (column-specification,...)

CREATE-VIEW-statement ::=
    CREATE VIEW <view name>
    [(<column name>, ...)]
    AS SELECT-statement

DELETE-statement ::=
    DELETE FROM <table name>
    [WHERE-clause]

DROP-statement ::=
    DROP <table name> : <view name> :
    <index name> alphanumeric-expression ::=
    alphanumeric-constant : columnID

GRANT-statement ::=
    GRANT system-privilege-level : access-privilege-level
    [ON <table name>]
    TO <user name>
    IDENTIFIED BY <password>

INSERT-statement ::=
    INSERT INTO <table name>
    [(<column name>, ...)]
    VALUES (<constant>, ...) :
    SELECT-statement

REVOKE-statement ::=
    REVOKE system-privilege-level : access-privilege-level
    [ON <table name>]
    FROM <user name>

SELECT-statement ::=
    SELECT * : column-expression
    FROM tableID,...
    [WHERE-clause]
    [GROUP BY columnID,...
    [HAVING condition :
    ORDER BY columnID,... [ASC:DESC]]

UPDATE-statement ::=
    UPDATE <table name>
    SET <column name> = expression
    [WHERE-clause]

 access-privilege-level ::=
    SELECT : UPDATE [(<column name>, ...)] : DELETE : ALL

arithmetic-expression ::=
    numeric-constant :
    columnID :
    arithmetic-expression arithmetic-operator arithmetic-expression :
    (arithmetic-expression)

arithmetic-operator ::=
  * : / : + : -

column-specification ::=
  <column name> data-type [NOT NULL]

comparison-operator ::=
  = : < : > : <= : >= : <>

condition ::=
  expression comparison-operator expression : expression comparison-
  operator subquery

columnID ::=
  <column name>:
  <table name>.<column name>:
  <alias> <column name>

column-expression ::=
  columnID:
  function

data-type ::=
  CHAR : NUMBER : DATE : LONG

expression ::=
  arithmetic-expression :
  alphanumeric-expression

function ::=
  COUNT : MIN : MAX : SUM : AVG
  (<column name>)

subquery :: =
  SELECT column-expression
  FROM tableID,...
  [WHERE condition]
  [GROUP BY columnID,... : HAVING condition]

system-privilege-level ::=
   CONNECT : DBA : RESOURCE

tableID ::=
   <table name>:
   <table name> <alias>:
   <view name>

WHERE-clause ::=
   WHERE condition

Appendix 3
Codd's Thirteen Rules

A3.1 An Evaluation Scheme

In the mid-1980s E.F. Codd published a theoretical assessment of the state of relational products in a number of papers (Codd, 1985). The structure of this discussion centred around 13 rules which Codd defined as an evaluation scheme for products claiming to be RDBMS. Since that time, Codd has extended the number of rules so that they now number in the hundreds (Codd, 1990). The 13 rules in the 1985 paper however still act as the foundation for Codd's definition of a relational DBMS. It must be said that no existing product satisfies all of the rules. Nevertheless, Codd's work is influential in that most RDBMS's are taking great strides to match their capabilities with Codd's ideal. It is for this reason that we consider them here.

The 13 rules are:

(0)   Foundation Rule
(1)   Information Rule
(2)   Guaranteed Access Rule
(3)   Systematic Nulls Rule
(4)   Dynamic Catalogue Rule
(5)   Comprehensive Data Sub-language Rule
(6)   View Updating Rule
(7)   High-level Language Rule
(8)   Physical Data Independence Rule
(9)   Logical Data Independence Rule
(10) Integrity Independence Rule
(11) Distribution Independence Rule
(12) Non-subversion Rule.

A3.2 Foundation Rule

The rules from 1 to 12 listed above are based on a single foundation rule which Codd calls rule zero. This rule states that any system which claims to be a relational database management system must be able to manage databases entirely through its relational capabilities.

This means that an RDBMS must support a data definition language, a data manipulation language, a data integrity language, and a data control language all of which must work at the level of relations. That is, a multiple-record at a time way of working (see section 1.7.2).

A3.3 Information Rule

All information in a relational database must be represented explicitly at the logical level in exactly one way, by values in tables (see section 2.2.2). Besides the foundation rule, this is probably the most important rule as far as Codd is concerned. DBMS that do not conform to this rule do not even get to play the game.

A3.4 Guaranteed Access Rule

Each and every item of data in a relational database must be guaranteed to be logically accessible by resorting to a combination of table name, primary key name and primary key value (see section 2.2.6).

A3.5 Systematic Nulls Rule

Null values (distinct from the empty character string, a string of blank characters, and distinct from zero or any other number) must be supported in a fully relational DBMS for representing missing and inapplicable information in a systematic way (see section 4.2.3).

A3.6 Dynamic Catalogue Rule

The description of the database must be represented at the logical level just like ordinary data. This means that authorised users can apply the same relational data manipulation language to its interrogation as they apply to ordinary data (see section 2.2.9).

A3.7 Comprehensive Data Sub-language Rule

A relational system must support at least one language which is comprehensive in supporting all of the following features (see section 1.8):

(1) Data definition

(2) View definition

(3) Data manipulation (interactive and by program)

(4) Integrity constraints

(5) Authorisation

(6) Transaction boundaries.

A3.8 View Updating Rule

All views that are theoretically updateable must be updateable in practice by the DBMS (see section 5.2.3).

A3.9 High-level Language Rule

The capability of handling a relation as a single operation applies not only to the retrieval of data, but also to the insertion, update and deletion of data. All such operations should be available not only in interactive mode but also via programming in some conventional host language (see sections 7.3 and 7.4).

A3.10 Physical Data Independence Rule

Application systems and terminal activities must remain logically unimpaired whenever changes are made either to storage structures or access methods.

In the relational approach the main concern is with the logical level. Most existing RDBMS handle data at the physical level in non-relational ways. What Codd is saying however is that if any changes are made to the way in which data is physically stored, perhaps to improve performance, then this should not affect in any way the logical view of such data (see appendix 1).

A3.11 Logical Data Independence Rule

Application systems and terminal activities must remain logically unimpaired when information-preserving changes of any kind are made to the base tables.

Codd is detailing here the need for a mechanism which buffers applications and end-users from such changes to base files as a split of a table for storage or performance reasons. This technique, much used in distributed database systems, is outside the scope of this book.

A3.12 Integrity Independence Rule

Integrity constraints specific to a database must be definable in the relational database sub-language and storable in the system catalogue, not in application programs (see section 4.4.1).

A3.13 Distribution Independence Rule

Application systems or terminal activities must be logically unimpaired by the re-distribution of data amongst various sites on a data communication network. This is a very difficult rule for any present DBMS to fulfil in its entirety. Distributed databases are however a prime topic of development for most major vendors and some progress has been made.

A3.14 Non-subversion Rule

If a relational system has a single-record-at-a-time language, that low-level of working must not be used to subvert or by-pass the integrity rules expressed in a higher-level relational language which employs a multiple-record-at-a-time method of processing.

Appendix 4
Goronwy Galvanising: A Case Study

A4.1 Background

Goronwy Galvanising is a small company specialising in treating steel products such as lintels, crash barriers, palisades, etc., produced by other manufacturers. Galvanising, in very simple terms, involves dipping steel products into baths of molten zinc to provide a rust-free coating. Untreated steel products are described as being black products. Treated products are referred to as being white products. There is a slight gain in weight as a result of the galvanising process.

Black products are delivered to Goronwy on large trailers. Each trailer carries a series of bundled products known as batches. A batch is made up of a number of steel products of the same type and is labelled with a unique job number. Each trailer may be loaded with a number of different types of steel product and is labelled with its own advice note detailing all the associated jobs on the trailer.

Blackheads Steel Products					Despatch Advice	
Advice No. *A3137*				**Date** *11-1-88*		
Customer & Address Goronwy Galvanising, Cardiff				**Instructions** *Galvanise & Return*		
Order Number	Description	Product Code	Item Length	Number This Delivery	Weight (tonnes)
13/1193G	*Lintels*		*1500*	*20*	
44/2404G			*1500*	*20*	
70/2517P			*1350*	*20*	
23/2474P			*1200*	*16*	
Hauliers Name *International 5*		**Received in Good Order and Sound Condition**			

Figure A4.1

Goronwy Galvanising					Despatch Advice		
Advice No. 101				**Date** 12/02/90			
Customer & Address Blackheads, Cardiff							
Order Number	**Description**	**Product Code**	**Item Length**	**Order Qty**	**Batch Weight**	**Returned Qty**	**Returned Weight**
13/1193G	Lintels	UL15	1500	20	150	20	150
44/2404G		UL15	1500	20	150	20	150
70/2517P		UL135	1350	20	135	20	135
23/2474P		UL12	1200	16	100	14	82
Driver			**Received By**				

Figure A4.2

Goronwy mainly process lintels for a major steel manufacturer, Blackheads. The advice note supplied with trailers of Blackhead's lintels is identified by an advice number specific to this manufacturer. Each job is identified on the advice note by a job number generated by Blackhead's own check-digit routine.

Smaller manufacturers like Pimples supply an advice note on which jobs are identified by a concatenation of the advice number and line number on which the job appears.

Each job, whether it be for Blackheads or Pimples, is also described on the advice note in terms of a product code, a product description, item length, order quantity and batch weight. Each advice is dated.

When Goronwy have treated a series of jobs they will stack white material on trailers ready to be returned to the associated manufacturers. Each trailer must have an associated advice note detailing material on the trailer. Partial despatches may be made from one job. This means that the trailer of white material for despatch need not correspond to the trailer of black material originally supplied to Goronwy. The despatch advice is given a unique advice number and is dated. Each despatch details the job number, product code, description, item length, batch weight, returned quantity and returned weight.

Figure A4.1 illustrates a delivery advice note received from Blackheads indicating black material on a trailer. Figure A4.2 illustrates a despatch advice note prepared by Goronwy for white material.

A4.2 Database Design

Our first task would be to analyse a history of such documentation, the aim being to plot the dependencies between the data items used by Goronwy.

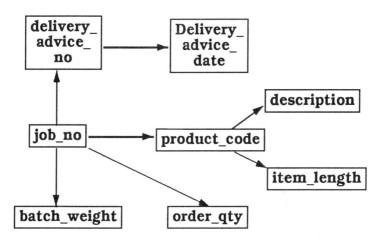

Figure A4.3

Figure A4.3 illustrates a determinancy diagram drawn from an analysis of delivery advices - the advice notes received from Blackheads and Pimples. Figure A4.4 illustrates a determinancy diagram drawn from an analysis of despatch advices - the advice notes produced by Goronwy.

Translating our determinancy diagram for delivery advices into table structures we arrive at the following schema:

Delivery_advices
(Delivery-Advice-no, Delivery_advice_date)
Jobs
(Job-no, Product_code, Batch_weight, Order_qty, Delivery_advice_no)
Products
(Product-code, description, Item_length)

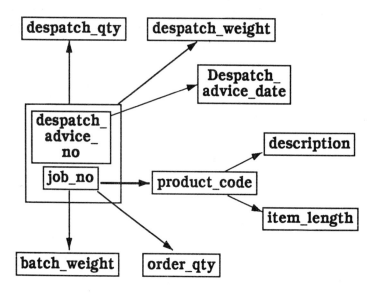

Figure A4.4

Likewise, translating our determinancy diagram for despatch advices into table structures we arrive at the following schema:

Jobs
(Job-no, Product_code, Batch_weight,Order_qty, Delivery_advice_no)
Products
(Product-code, description, Item_length)
Despatch_advices
(Despatch-advice-no, Despatch_advice_date)
Despatches
(Despatch-advice-no, Job-no, Despatch_qty, Despatch_weight)

Combining the two schemas we arrive at the following database design for the business of Goronwy Galvanising:

Jobs
(Job-no, Product_code, Batch_weight,Order_qty, Delivery_advice_no)
Products
(Product-code, description, Item_length)

Despatch_advices
(Despatch-advice-no,Despatch_advice_date)
Delivery_advices
(Delivery_advice_no, Delivery_advice_date)
Despatches
(Despatch-advice-no, Job-no, Despatch_qty, Despatch_weight)

A4.3 Implementing the Design

For each of the table structures in our schema we produce a create table
statement in SQL:

```
CREATE TABLE delivery_advices
     (delivery_no CHAR(5) NOT NULL,
      delivery_date DATE, NOT NULL)

CREATE TABLE despatch_advices
     (despatch_no CHAR(5) NOT NULL,
      despatch_date DATE, NOT NULL)

CREATE TABLE jobs
     (job_no CHAR(9) NOT NULL,
      delivery_no CHAR(5) NOT NULL,
      product_code CHAR(9) NOT NULL,
      order_qty NUMBER(5) NOT NULL,
      batch_weight NUMBER(7,2))

CREATE TABLE products
     (product_code CHAR(9) NOT NULL,
      description CHAR(20),
      item_length NUMBER(5) NOT NULL)

CREATE TABLE despatches
     (despatch_no CHAR(5) NOT NULL,
      job_no CHAR(9) NOT NULL,
      despatch_qty NUMBER(5) NOT NULL,
      despatch_weight NUMBER(7,2) NOT NULL)
```

Note that we have abbreviated some of the data item names , such as delivery_advice_no to delivery_no, for convenience. Note also we have specified quite a few more not null constraints than are strictly necessary for inherent integrity reasons. Declaring a data item such as despatch_qty to be not null however is a fundamental business rule here. We must always record the amount of a job despatched back to the manufacturer.

To be entirely accurate, our implementation as it presently stands is not entirely as clean as it should be. One area we might address is the nature of any derived values in our scheme. Clearly, for instance, the weight of a particular batch can be calculated from the weight of any unit of a particular type of product multiplied by the order quantity. The same reasoning applies to the calculation of a despatch weight. We therefore choose to modify our database structure slightly by including a unit weight field in the products table and removing the two derived fields.

Another modification concerns the way in which the data will be used in Goronwy. Since partial despatches can be made from each job, the production controller at Goronwy regularly has to know how much material is still left on site. Clearly the quantity outstanding for any particular job can be calculated by deducting the total quantity despatched from the original order quantity. For performance reasons however we choose to introduce some redundancy into our scheme by placing a quantity out-standing field in the jobs record. Our modified structure is given below:

```
CREATE TABLE delivery_advices
     (delivery_no CHAR(5) NOT NULL,
      delivery_date DATE, NOT NULL)


CREATE TABLE despatch_advices
     (despatch_no CHAR(5) NOT NULL,
      despatch_date DATE, NOT NULL)


CREATE TABLE jobs
     (job_no CHAR(9) NOT NULL,
      delivery_no CHAR(5) NOT NULL,
      product_code CHAR(9) NOT NULL,
      order_qty NUMBER(5) NOT NULL,
      out_qty NUMBER(5))
```

```
CREATE TABLE products
     (product_code CHAR(9) NOT NULL,
      description CHAR(20),
      item_length NUMBER(5) NOT NULL
      unit_weight NUMBER(7,2) NOT NULL)

CREATE TABLE despatches
     (despatch_no CHAR(5) NOT NULL,
      job_no CHAR(9) NOT NULL,
      despatch_qty NUMBER(5) NOT NULL)
```

The next step is to enforce entity integrity via a series of unique indexes as follows:

```
CREATE UNIQUE INDEX delivery_ind
ON delivery_advices(delivery_no)

CREATE UNIQUE INDEX despatch_ind
ON despatch_advices(despatch_no)

CREATE UNIQUE INDEX job_ind
ON jobs(job_no)

CREATE UNIQUE INDEX product_ind
ON products(product_code)

CREATE UNIQUE INDEX despatches_ind
ON despatches(despatch_no, job_no)
```

Finally, we can prime the tables with the initial data-set via a series of insert statements. For example, we can prime the delivery_advices table as follows:

```
INSERT INTO delivery_advices
VALUES
('A3137','11-JAN-90')
```

INSERT INTO delivery_advices
VALUES
('A3138','11-JAN-90')

INSERT INTO delivery_advices
VALUES
('A3139','12-JAN-90')

INSERT INTO delivery_advices
VALUES
('A3140','12-JAN-90')

A4.4 Implementing Views

Suppose we have a regular requirement to join the delivery_advices table
and the jobs table together to recompose the information received on the
original paper advices. The easiest way to achieve this is via a view such as
the one outlined below.

```
CREATE VIEW deliveries AS
SELECT D.delivery_no, D.delivery_date, J.job_no,
        J.product_code, order_qty, unit_weight,
        (order_qty * unit_weight) batch_weight
FROM delivery_advices D, jobs J, products P
WHERE D.delivery_no = J.delivery_no
  AND J.product_code = P.product_code;
```

Note how we use a function in the select clause to generate a pseudo-
column which we have named batch_weight.

A4.5 Creating Reports

Any database is created for a purpose. In the case of Goronwy Galvanising,
the primary purpose is to improve the monitoring of the production
process. A whole range of standard reports can hence be produced to fulfil
this objective. We detail an SQL script for one such report below:

TTITLE 'List of Jobs by Delivery Advice';
COLUMN delivery_no HEADING 'Delivery:Number' FORMAT A10;
COLUMN delivery_date HEADING 'Delivery:Date' FORMAT A10;
COLUMN job_no HEADING 'Job:Number' FORMAT A8;
COLUMN product_code HEADING 'Product:Code' FORMAT A8;
COLUMN batch_weight HEADING '
Batch:Weight' FORMAT 999999999;
COLUMN order_qty HEADING 'Order:Qty' FORMAT 99999;
BREAK ON delivery_no SKIP 1;
SELECT delivery_no, delivery_date, job_no, product_code, batch_weight
FROM deliveries
ORDER BY delivery_no, job_no;

This report uses the view established in the previous section to detail for the user all jobs associated with particular delivery advices.

A4.6 Suggested Improvements

We have only indicated the skeleton of a database system for Goronwy Galvanising in the discussion above. The aim has been to give an illustration of the process of building a relational database system for a given company need. One much-needed extra would be a user-interface of menus and data-entry screens, perhaps constructed using tools such as ORACLE's SQL*Forms and SQL*Menus. We indicate below a series of suggested improvements to the system which can be treated as exercises for the reader.

(1) Produce a report which will list all associated despatches on despatch advice notes. Note that despatch_weight is now a derived field. We suggest you therefore create a view for despatches first.
(2) Produce a report which will list all completed jobs. In other words, all jobs where the quantity outstanding is set to zero.
(3) Produce a report listing all products information on file in order of product code.
(4) Produce a statement which will regularly remove all completed jobs information from the system.
(5) Produce a view of all products information presently unused in the system.

Index